THE EASY ELECTRIC COOKBOOK

THE EASY ELECTRIC COOKBOOK

NINA FROUD

Produced in collaboration with The Electricity Council

HEINEMANN·LONDON

William Heinemann Ltd
15 Queen Street, Mayfair,
London W1X 8BE

LONDON MELBOURNE
TORONTO JOHANNESBURG
AUCKLAND

Illustrations by
Victoria Franklin

Photographs by Bill
Richmond (Nucleus Studios)
pages 35–45/48/52–54/
62–68/94–106/124

Designed by Philip Mann

Filmset and Printed by
Jarrold and Sons Ltd,
Norwich

CONTENTS

Acknowledgments
I should like to express my gratitude to Anthony Byers for his help with suggestions on lighting and for supplying many of the illustrations for this book; to Pelham Books for permission to quote from Anthony Byers's book *Home Lighting*; to Robert Cotton for undertaking a great deal of the research for this book; to Gwen Conacher, Home Economist of the Electricity Council Marketing Department, for her excellent information on freezers; to Monica Wilkins for much valuable assistance; and to Kathleen Tranmar for breaking even her own record in getting the manuscript ready.

Nina Froud

The publishers are, in addition, most grateful to the various manufacturers who kindly made their equipment available for photographing.

For the convenience of users of this book, ingredients are given in both the Imperial and the metric systems. These are not always straight conversions: suitable adjustments have been made and the reason for this is explained below.

The complete change-over to the metric system in Great Britain will be gradual and will be completed by 1978. Many industries have already adopted it. Kitchen units and utensils of the future will be in metric sizes and all the food which we buy will be sold in metric weights and measures.

The United Kingdom Federation for Education in Home Economics, to help us to adjust to metrication, have taken 25 grams as the basic unit. Several good reasons are given for the selection of this unit of weight. It is easily multiplied for larger metric quantities – 50 – 100 – 250 – 500. It provides the foundation for *thinking metrically* to carry us beyond the stage of trying to convert Imperial weights into their exact and awkward metric equivalents, e.g. 100 g as an easy alternative to 4 oz.

Many recipes are based on proportions, such as 'half fat to flour' or one part fat and one part flour to ten parts liquid for a sauce; these are easily calculated if the basic unit is chosen sensibly.

In all recipes in this book I have, accordingly, adopted 25 g as the basic metric unit of weight.

But I ought to say a word on why approximate conversions between Imperial and metric units have been used. Thankfully, few recipes are such that a cook has to follow them with the extreme precision called for in a chemical laboratory. If you say 'roll out pastry to a thickness of $\frac{1}{4}$ inch' you expect the housewife to judge that thickness by eye. It would be rather absurd, therefore, to include a solemn metric equivalent of 6·35 millimetres (which, in fact, it is) because this would require at least an engineer's micrometer to measure it. A suitable round figure for the metric user is 5 mm (again judged by eye) and this is the kind of metric conversion I have made throughout. A convenient list is given here for reference.

The change-over to metric does not mean that we can't use any of the existing and often much-loved pots and pans and baking tins. All we shall need to do is to convert the size from inches to the nearest round millimetre, as is already done in this book. Thus the 7 in. cake tin is merely rechristened an 18 cm tin.

MEASURES AND METRICATION

Imperial measures

16 ounces (oz)	1 pound (lb)
12 inches (in.)	1 foot (ft)
4 gills	1 pint
2 pints	1 quart
4 quarts	1 gallon

ALSO

20 fluid ounces	1 pint

Metric measures

1,000 grams (g)	1 kilogram (kg)
10 millimetres (mm)	1 centimetre (cm)
100 centimetres or 1,000 millimetres	1 metre (m)
1,000 cubic centimetres (cm³) or millilitres (ml)	1 litre (L)

Approximate conversions

Weight

1 ounce	25 grams
2 oz	50 g
4 oz	100 g
8 oz	200 g
12 oz	300 g
1 lb	500 g ($\frac{1}{2}$ kg)
2 lb	1 kilogram

Capacity

1 gill ($\frac{1}{4}$ pint)	125 millilitres
$\frac{1}{2}$ pint	250 ml
1 pint	500 ml ($\frac{1}{2}$ litre)
1 quart (2 pints)	1 litre

A tablespoon is equivalent to $\frac{1}{2}$ oz, say 15 g.
A teaspoon is equivalent to one-sixth of an ounce, say 5 g.
Measuring jugs for use with water, cream, wine, etc., are often marked in (fluid) ounces. In the recipes 4 oz (100 ml) can be taken as $\frac{1}{4}$ pint or 1 gill.

OVEN TEMPERATURE

Another result of using metric in our kitchens is that the calibration of thermostats on electric ovens will be changed. At present they are calibrated in intervals of 25 °F. From 1975 they are to be calibrated with marks every 10 °Celsius (Centigrade).

Here is the table of approximate equivalent temperatures as recommended by the Association of Manufacturers of Domestic Electrical Appliances.

Present scale °Fahrenheit	Recommended conversion to °Celsius scale
200 °F	100 °C
225 °F	110 °C
250 °F	130 °C
275 °F	140 °C
300 °F	150 °C
325 °F	170 °C
350 °F	180 °C
375 °F	190 °C
400 °F	200 °C
425 °F	220 °C
450 °F	230 °C
475 °F	240 °C
500 °F	250 °C

As you can see the two most commonly used settings 350 °F and 425 °F are converted to 180 °C (i.e. 356 °F) and 220 °C (i.e. 428 °F).

If you glance at the comparative scale above, you will see that the 100 °F settings, from 200 °F on, are halved in the new 100 °C settings, i.e. 200 °F = 100 °C, etc.

For the change-over, no doubt, all electric cooker manufacturers will supply conversion charts, and we shall take it all in our stride.

In the meantime, users of this book need not worry about temperature conversions. Oven temperatures in all recipes are given in both Fahrenheit and Celsius.

In many modern homes, in our servantless times, the kitchen, quite rightly, is the centre of family living. This means the kitchen has to be not only an efficient place for cooking the meals, but also a pleasant room to sit in.

Living space generally continues to contract: the average home unit is smaller, so using what room there is to best possible advantage becomes a priority. The kitchen must be arranged and equipped in such a way as to please one visually and make the business of cooking for one's family or guests an enjoyable experience. So much can be done to brighten up the most unpromising of kitchens.

My own started off with every possible built-in disadvantage. It is too small and the shape, flaunting its former music-hall ancestry, defies any recognizable geometrical definition. A kind friend once called it a 'hexagonal rectangle'.

My young daughter, when she first saw the kitchen, immediately condemned 'the view' from my window. She said it looked like a public lavatory. Well . . . it is a blank wall completely covered with white tiles . . . from the ground to the fifth floor – as far as the eye can see.

My walls, wherever there is enough straight flat surface, are covered with peg board, on which hang all the gadgets I use. I can see them at a glance and need not chip my nail varnish rummaging in a drawer. The offending panorama is successfully screened off with some glass shelves on which I keep pot plants. Some are herbs for eating, others trail down for camouflage. It works. No one has ever noticed the white tiled wall.

My kitchen also had an awkward door. A menace whichever way it opened. When it was hung so as to open inwards, it halved the size of the tiny eating space. When it was changed to open outwards, it threatened to knock out anyone coming out of the bathroom. We did the only thing we could with that door: banished it to the cellar.

I dislike being cut off from my friends while I am in the kitchen, so I had a window cut into the living room. This acts as a serving hatch but, what is more important, it is also my means of communication – by sound and vision – with my guests.

My favourite meals are brunches and suppers I can share with close friends in the kitchen. More than three guests in my kitchen would turn what should be attractive informality into cramped discomfort. The rule of the house, therefore, is that, however informal the meal, if there are more than four people, we eat in the living room. One thing I must add in defence of my kitchen. In spite of its size, it doesn't prevent me from having twelve or sixteen guests for dinner, when the spirit moves me.

Of course, no one will dispute the advantages of a well-planned kitchen. You can save yourself an awful lot of walking if your storage and equipment is readily accessible. Ideally, every appliance should have its place and be ready for use whenever it is needed. A properly planned kitchen should be well lit (and I shall return to the subject of lighting later), well ventilated, have enough socket outlets for all the appliances.

It should have enough storage space and uncluttered surfaces. This makes it easy to keep tidy. The floor covering should also be of a kind that is simple to clean.

Ideas for the kitchen

Most of us have our own ideas on what is a well-equipped kitchen. My own needs tend to be unorthodox. Because I have a demanding full-time job, much of my cooking – except at weekends – is done at night. Lighting which suits my needs, therefore, is as important to me in the kitchen as in my study. One must be able to see what is happening in a saucepan or a mixing bowl, especially when making preparations in which textures are important. This applies to many things, from sauces to home-made sweets.

We can't, alas, all be lucky enough to have our kitchens planned from the start. Most of the time we have to settle for whatever space and plumbing allows. Often we can't even prevent the cooker being in the darkest corner of the kitchen. But we can remedy a lot by insisting on the kind of lighting we want.

A lot of people still have larders. Personally I am always a bit suspicious about the efficiency of larders – except possibly in Siberia. However cool and airy and well ventilated, I'd probably keep nothing but cheese and eggs in it, if I had one. No, come to think of it, if I had one, I would use the space for an extra refrigerator.

The planning and equipment of kitchens has been exercising home advisers for centuries.

A list of equipment considered indispensable in the 1530s in the kitchen of Château La Motte – after richly worked silver chafing dishes – included such items as six big copper candlesticks and 'one deep copper basin for washing hands'.

As late as 1914, the most famous and successful best-selling cookery book author – a Russian – brought out a work which purported to help a housewife of modest means to plan her kitchen. She insisted that it was absolutely essential for the kitchen to be 'near' for two considerations:

'*Moral consideration* – The morals of the servants are bound to improve, if you plan the kitchen on the same floor as the living rooms.

'*Economic consideration* – If the kitchen is near, so that one can get from a warm pantry to the cold cellar, then the mistress of the house, if she be of delicate health, can have the convenience of the warm pantry to supervise the allocation of food supplies for the day. Nothing extra would get sneaked past her.'

Not much attention is given to the actual planning of the kitchen itself. There are only two specifications: 'the baking oven must be big enough to take four logs and the hood over the stove must have sufficient clearance to prevent one banging one's head and knocking oneself out'.

Much more a man after my own heart is Michel Chevalier. In *Magazin Pittoresque*, a fashionable French journal in the 1840s, he wrote: 'The improvement of household utensils has more to do with real freedom than is generally realized, for it contributes a great deal to freedom from drudgery in the home, which matters no less to human happiness than liberty in a public place.' Who would quarrel with that?

He goes on: 'One utensil may free the servants from one type of arduous or unhealthy task, another allows one person to do the work of three and, consequently, frees two from domestic slavery.' Substitute 'house-wife' for 'servants' and it all applies today, with the pressing need to combat the ever-increasing demand on our time.

Marshal the right appliances in your kitchen in the logical sequence for the way you feel your work ideally should be done – and you have an easy electric kitchen. How do you set about it?

If money is no problem, you can have your kitchen altered completely, redesign it to suit your particular requirements. If the transformation of your kitchen, to suit your needs and taste, involves building as well as redesigning, consult an architect.

If you have to do it on a shoe-string, you can still

work miracles, with a bit of skill and ingenuity and some help from do-it-yourself shops. These shops, catering for the handyman, can supply all the necessary tools and materials. Many of the materials are neither prohibitively expensive nor difficult to use. You can get kitchen units in kits, which are economical and easy to assemble.

The choice of kitchen units is enormous, as will be seen from the illustrations.

You should insist that the kitchen furniture is so arranged as to give you ample space for all your appliances and to provide you with enough storage space. Your kitchen furniture doesn't have to be all modern. The old and the new can live together in great harmony. Make the most of any good feature; use colour and shape to create a comfortable atmosphere and style which reflects your personality.

Professional advice

Whether you can afford to pay for substantial structural alterations or are disposed to do the job of modernizing your kitchen yourself, you would do well to study design requirements as specified by the National House Building Council. The address is 58 Portland Place, London W1M 4BU.

Another valuable document for prospective kitchen planners to study is the British Standard recommendations. This is the revision of BS 3705:1964, and to obtain the text, apply to the British Standards Institution, 2 Park Street, London W1A 2BS. For other help bear in mind that Electricity Boards will give advice on fitting appliances and some have a kitchen planning service.

Let us imagine that there are no obstacles and plenty of money: what are the main things to aim for in planning an ideal kitchen?

The National House Building Council advocates that, first of all, there must be a clear space not less than 600 millimetres in width (that's about 2 feet) to include the necessary pipes and cables for the cooker. This space must not be under a window, which is sensible advice from the point of view of safety. If you have a cooker under a window, there is a danger of kitchen curtains catching fire.

The kitchen should have a sink with at least one draining board. Twin sinks and two draining boards are even better. The sink unit must be at least 1 metre (39 inches) wide. There should be space for work surfaces on each side of the sink and on each side of the cooker.

There should be two clear spaces for storage or for other appliances. One of these spaces should be at least 600 mm and the other 800 mm wide (say, 2 ft and 2 ft 8 in.).

All of the above are compulsory requirements and most builders accept them. In addition, the Council makes further recommendations for increased convenience and safety. One of the recommendations, for example, is that whenever possible there should be a clearance of at least 300 mm (1 ft) on both sides of the cooker.

There are various recommendations for the 'correct' height of working surfaces and storage levels. I must say I don't believe there is any such thing as 'correct' height. What might be a comfortable height for a 6 ft 2 in. man would be torture for a 5 ft 2 in. woman. You are planning your kitchen: the heights of all work tops and furniture should be absolutely right for you.

Making a plan
Having digested all the information you have collected, set about making the plan of your kitchen. Take a careful measurement of the walls. Draw up the plan to scale, giving height of your kitchen and length of walls. Show the position and width of doors and windows, as well as water pipes and drains. Now work out possible arrangements of basic layouts.

Decide in which basic category the layout of your kitchen most obviously fits, and use it as a guide for your plan of your own requirements. Compare the siting of the cooker, sink, refrigerator, food freezer, dish washer, waste disposer, the storage cupboards, etc.

Be as generous as you can with work surfaces and plan for appliances such as food mixer, blender, coffee grinder, and whatever else you are likely to have ready at hand. If you can't spare surface space for these very useful 'kitchen maids', arrange for them to be stored so that you can get them out easily.

The range of appliances, small and large, which simplify and speed repetitive jobs, is enormous and I shall deal with the more important ones in detail.

In writing this book it is not my intention to lay down the law. I merely hope to provide some ideas for people who want to make the most of their kitchen. In the end, you yourself must decide what would be useful and desirable.

For my part, if in planning my ideal kitchen I should run into money difficulties, which is more than likely, and have to make a sacrifice somewhere, I know what I would do. I would give up the idea of those gorgeous hand-painted tiles, rather than do without my dish washer.

Let us come back for a moment to the difficulty of suggesting which particular supplementary appliances one should have in the kitchen, once one has the essentials installed. How, for instance, does one assess whether one needs a vegetable peeler? One suggestion is to calculate the number of woman-hours you spend peeling potatoes and multiply it by whatever you feel your rate per hour should be. If the gadget justifies itself over a year, it is worth buying. One thing I feel strongly about: for a busy professional woman, or a mother with a family to cater for, all labour- and time-saving equipment is not a luxury but a social need. I think Women's Lib started not so much with the ceremonial burning of the often much-needed bra, but with the coming of labour-saving devices which freed us from time-consuming chores.

I'm not being flippant. If we go back only 50, or even 30, years, never mind the Victorian era, and look at the life of the majority of women in the most advanced countries, like Britain, the changes are tremendous.

The end of drudgery

Contrary to popular belief, women have gone out to work all through the ages. Most could not afford to think of a job as something interesting, or something they wanted to do. It was invariably a question of necessity. And her work was truly never done. On returning from work, there was no chance for her to put up her feet and retreat behind the sports page of a newspaper. She had the shopping and the cooking, the cleaning and the laundering to do, after her paid job was done.

This sort of existence did not do the woman or her children any good. The mothers were worn out by the sheer drudgery which was their lot.

What a chore the washday must have been – all that soaking, and coppers on the boil. Antique shops nowadays do a fair trade in mothers' irons' – the kind you had to start off like a coal fire, with paper, sticks, charcoal, bellows, and all! Then, when it decided to get hot enough to iron clothes, you had to be careful not to make any sudden movement, almost not breathing, to prevent the iron gushing out soot and ashes on your freshly washed linen. Washing machines, driers, and electric irons have changed all that. A woman can put her washing into a machine and do what she likes while the machine gets on with making the linen clean. Dish washers have taken the drudgery out of washing up – one of the most uninspiring household jobs.

Electric hair driers make it possible to wash one's hair at any time, without catching one's death of cold, in climates where a suitable sunny Sunday afternoon may not occur more than three or four times a year. Vacuum cleaners have done away with housemaid's knee. Electric blankets are far from bricks heated in the fireplace, or hot-water bottles.

The greatest revolution, however, has taken place in the most important place of all – the kitchen. Modern electrical appliances are now available at a cost most of us who work can afford. They not only help to perform many otherwise tedious and time-consuming tasks quickly and easily, they increase our leisure for better things.

Electrical equipment

As you read through this book you will see that, in addition to cookers, I have devoted sections to many other electrical appliances. These are things I wouldn't be without and which I seem to spend my life intro-ducing to kitchens in homes from India to Italy.

One is a refrigerator, and a whole section later is devoted to dishes which can be made in a refrigerator, covering complete menus, including starting courses, soups, main courses, and desserts.

Another is a quick-boiling electric kettle. That is one of the great contributions we shall make to the Com-mon Market countries. I've been in so many elegant, well-equipped continental kitchens, where they have never heard of a real kettle. I have witnessed hilari-ously primitive arrangements for making tea, with spoutless saucepans spilling boiling water everywhere except into the teapot.

Others on my list of desirable equipment that is not prohibitively expensive are toasters which don't have to be watched, food mixers, blenders, and some of their attachments such as grinders and graters.

My attitude to food is absolutely uncompromising and I tend to foam at the mouth when told that a tube or packet of concentrate diluted in water is every bit as good a soup as mother used to make, or that some chemical concoction can be hastily whipped up into a delectable sweet.

I don't want to get leisure at the expense of eating sub-standard rubbish. What I do want is to be able to present wholesome and attractive dishes quickly, without spending hours shredding, sieving, pounding, chopping, stirring, and whisking till my arms feel like falling off.

I also expect my equipment to justify itself by saving me money. A blender is a great help in turning left-overs into smooth and creamy soups in minutes. It is invaluable for purées of all kinds, such as baby foods, which otherwise involve a lot of sieving and mashing, and for making fruit drinks and sauces. A mixer in the kitchen is a great boon, provided you observe the manufacturer's instructions – and use the right speeds for the right operations. Creaming fat and sugar for cakes, emulsifying mayonnaise, beating egg whites and batters, kneading pastry, etc. – all these are done by the mixer quickly and efficiently. Many owners use their mixers or blenders to make pleasant beauty preparations – from cucumber and honey face-masks and almond-oil hand lotions to moisturizers and deodorants.

There are shredding attachments which make it simple to produce a julienne of vegetables for soups, casseroles, salads, or garnishes: Cheese for sauces can be grated or shredded in no time, without catching your nails and knuckles on the grater.

I keep two grinders, one strictly for grinding coffee – and coffee does taste better freshly ground for each making – the other for everything else – breadcrumbs, nuts, hard cheese, sugar, and other hard ingredients. You can turn ordinary granulated sugar into finest powder for sprinkling on cakes in 5 seconds flat.

For the busy woman who has to find presentable meals in a hurry there are many other aids to quick cooking. There is a rotisserie for spit roasting, which doubles up as a spare oven, grill, and plate warmer. In an interesting way this 'modern' appliance is a nice throw-back to the early classical method of spit roasting meat, fish, and other food by rotating it over a source of heat.

I have tried out a very good and convenient deep fat fryer, thermostatically controlled to keep the oil at or below 375 °F (190 °C), which prevents overheating and fumes, and is very safe. It is free-standing (and therefore need not take up space on the cooker which at times can be crowded) and it is guaranteed splatter-proof. Excellent for whitebait, doughnuts, fritters of all kinds, and of course – chips. A friend who lives on a farm swears by her electric vegetable peeler. She has to cater for hefty appetites and uses, by my standard, a vast amount of potatoes for every meal – more than I use in a week. The other piece of kitchen equipment she is proud of is an electric can opener. As I don't like canned food, I cannot share her enthusiasm.

She laughed at my electric carving knife as the ultimate in decadence until she watched me deal with my Christmas turkey, which was boned and stuffed. All I had to do was to slice it like a sausage, which enabled me to serve sixteen people without letting anyone's food get cold.

The freezer

I have left the most important piece of equipment to the last, because it deserves to be in a class by itself – the freezer. Frozen foods are gaining in popularity, and while many people regularly buy various types of frozen products, ownership of food freezers is by no means so widespread. It is understandable that people are bound to hesitate before indulging in what they imagine to be an expensive and bulky piece of equipment. My own prejudice against freezers in the home is that unless one is sensible in one's approach, one may well end up by never eating anything fresh. I remember staying in a frighteningly prosperous home with a huge orchard and garden. There were marvellous baby carrots, beautiful peas, and other delectable vegetables and fruit. The produce was picked daily, but none was served. We were glumly chewing our way through packets harvested the year before. I swore I would never own a freezer and would avoid eating with people who were fanatical about theirs.

It has taken quite a time for me to outgrow this prejudice. Now, I say to myself, this is not a deity into which all the nicest and freshest food has to be fed to propitiate it, but just a piece of kitchen equipment. Its job is to serve me: to store foods as well as to preserve them indefinitely. It should lead to economies in money and time. If you grow a lot of garden produce, enjoy as much of it fresh as you can and freeze the surplus. If you live in a town, take advantage of a glut on the market when some fruit or vegetable is particularly cheap – asparagus, strawberries. Many firms supply food in bulk to freezer owners, which is invariably cheaper. Think also of the fares, time, and energy expended on daily shopping.

By making your freezer work for you, you can bring about a tremendous saving in time. There is a simple method called 'eat one – freeze two'. This means you make your favourite pie or casserole, tripling the ingredients. The amount of cooking and washing up of utensils is no greater than for one meal, but this method gives you a reserve of two more meals to be thawed and reheated as and when required. This principle is very useful in catering for a large party. You can do all your preparations at any time of day or night, days ahead, and freeze the dishes until needed. You will find recipes suitable for this treatment later in the book.

I'm one of the 'better safe than sorry' brigade, and before buying any article of electrical equipment I always look for this circular mark:

It means that an identical sample to the model I am inspecting has been successfully tested for safety in the Appliance Testing Laboratories of the Electricity Council, and awarded the seal of approval for electrical safety by the British Electrotechnical Approvals Board (BEAB).

Whenever I can I select my electrical goods from one of the 1,200 shops owned by Electricity Boards, not only because all their appliances carry the safety mark, but for other very practical reasons.

Consider the facts. All domestic electrical appliances bought from Electricity Boards are guaranteed for one year. If any part fails within this time the Boards will not only replace it but will also fit it free of charge. If you buy an appliance in one area and use it in another, or if you move house, the local Board will honour the guarantee. Expert help on all electrical matters is yours for the asking. Credit facilities and hire purchase terms are offered on all appliances and central heating. Furthermore, promotions and premium offers often enable you to obtain your requirements at reduced prices.

FUSES AND PLUGS

There is a limit to the amount of current which can pass through any wire or flex. Beyond this limit heat develops and damage to the insulation occurs causing a breakdown. Thus all domestic circuits are fitted with fuses: the fuse is a deliberate weak spot designed to fail as soon as the circuit becomes overloaded.

It is vital always to fit a fuse of the correct rating for a particular appliance or circuit. Never ever replace a fuse with another of higher rating or with some substitute such as a hairpin or a paper clip as this could cause the Electricity Board's main fuse to blow. Should this happen only a Board electrician can replace it.

About fuses

The recommended electric wiring for households these days uses plugs labelled '13 A'. This is shorthand for 13 amperes, the unit in which electric current is measured: most electricians call it '13 amps'.

The two most common types of fuse for household circuits are the rewirable and the cartridge. The rewirable type has a porcelain fuse bridge for the fuse wire and fits into a fuse holder installed in fuseboards or consumer units near the meter. Cartridge fuses are the sort found in the standard 13 A rectangular-pin plugs and some consumer units and switch fuses. They cannot be rewired.

All fused plugs are sold containing 13 A fuses. Therefore if a plug is to be used for an appliance of less than 700 W rating, such as a table lamp, the 13 A fuse (coloured brown) should be replaced by a 3 A cartridge (colour red). The only exception is the TV set, which needs a 13 A cartridge fuse in the plug.

Large fixed appliances, such as cookers and water heaters, have either a 30 A rewirable fuse on a main switch and fuse unit, or a high ruptive capacity (HRC) cartridge or rewirable fuse in the consumer unit.

There are also the new miniature circuit breakers now used more and more in new houses and flats. Looking like ordinary switches, they automatically flick themselves off if any circuit is overloaded or if a fault in an appliance fails to blow the plug or socket fuse. Instead of the troublesome business of rewiring a porcelain fuse, the circuit can be brought back into use simply by pressing the switch to the 'on' position.

First, of course, find and disconnect the appliance causing trouble. But even if you don't all that will happen is that the switch will flick off again. There is no danger of the wrong fuse wire being connected and there is better fire-risk protection because these circuit breakers are more sensitive than porcelain fuses. No skill is needed to reset a faulty circuit. You can see immediately which circuit has failed without having to take out the fuse holders.

Miniature circuit breakers are made in various different sizes and a consumer unit can be fitted with any combination to suit the installation. The circuit breaker can easily be removed from the unit for complete safety when working on a circuit. One kind has a push button instead of a switch, but works in exactly the same way.

Mending a Fuse

How do you find a fuse which has blown? A fuse will blow because the circuit is overloaded, because the fuse wire is of too low a rating, or because a fault in the wiring or an appliance causes either a short-circuit or a fault to earth.

A ring-circuit fuse will blow if there is a fault in the circuit wiring itself or if the circuit is overloaded because too many appliances are being used on it at once.

The first thing to do when a fuse fails is to correct the condition which caused the failure. Switch off or disconnect any appliance that you suspect may have caused the trouble. Switch off the main switch before removing any fuses from the fuseboard. If you are not sure which circuit is faulty in a traditional wiring system, switch off all the main switches. Examine each fuse in turn, by the light of a torch if necessary, until you find one which has broken or melted fuse wire.

Here's how to rewire the fuse. Unscrew the terminal screws on the fuse holder and remove the broken wire. Clean any melted metal and scorch marks off the fuse holder.

Replace the fuse wire with a piece of the same rating: 15 A for lighting circuits, 10 or 15 A for power circuits, and 30 A for ring mains or large fixed appliances. Wind the new wire round one terminal post. Wind clockwise, otherwise the wire tends to unwind as the screw is tightened. Screw the wire down. Run the wire across to the other terminal post, wind it round clockwise again, and screw down. Do not stretch the wire tight between the terminal posts. Replace the fuse holder in the box, close the box, and switch on the main switch. Your appliance should now work again.

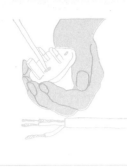

Wiring a plug

It is quite easy to wire a 13 A plug on the end of a flex. Carefully strip 2 in. (50 mm) of sheathing from the flex. Tape or sleeve the end if the flex is braided. Clamp the end of the unstripped flex in the plug's cord grip.

The *brown* wire is run to a live pin, marked L; the *blue* wire to a neutral pin, marked N; and the *green/yellow* earth wire to the earth pin, marked E or 1.

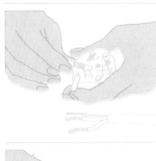

You will probably need to cut the wires so they reach the terminals without spare cable. Leave about $\frac{3}{8}$ in. (9 mm) for fixing to the terminal, then strip away this much insulation and insert the bare wires into the holes provided (or twist it clockwise to tighten on the simple screw type). Now tighten the screws on the terminals and check for stray strands, which should be removed.

Insert the correct cartridge fuse. This is 3 A – coloured red – for appliances of less than 700 watts, such as lamps, radio, and electric blankets. It is 13 A – coloured brown – for appliances rated at more than 700 W. Screw up the back of the plug and you are ready to test the appliance.

But do read the instruction booklet supplied with the appliance. Many people seem so eager to try out their new electrical helper that they cannot hold back their impatience and they could damage themselves and the appliance.

The Electricity Board maintain a 24-hour emergency service if you run into trouble. Keep the phone number handy – or you can look it up in your telephone directory under 'Electricity'.

As mentioned, I shall be writing about a number of the most important electrical appliances, as well as suggesting many recipes for their use. But here I want to say something about kitchen lighting and power sockets.

When I first moved into my present awkwardly shaped kitchen, there was a single bulb hanging from the ceiling, shedding an unwilling light on that part of the room furthest away from the working area. The first thing I did was to install a fluorescent fitting on the ceiling and paint the kitchen white. That made all the difference.

There are many times when a cook needs to have a clear view of what is going on in saucepans, and I have been in a kitchen where the lady of the house kept on checking the texture of her sauce by removing the pan from the heat and inspecting it under the one source of light.

I cannot emphasize the importance of lighting too much in the kitchen, for deficient lighting can cause one to ruin a dish. I remember such an occasion in what the estate agent would describe as a 'luxury flat'. It certainly reflected the personalities and civilized taste of the owners. The living room was furnished with flair, there were lots of books, good paintings, flowers – and such clever lighting! At the touch of a knob, the main lights could be dimmed and there was a profusion of table lamps.

Yet that night the main course, a beautiful and expensive salmon trout, tasted like a cross between foam rubber and straw matting. It was ruined by being boiled too fast on too high a heat, instead of being simmered gently and lovingly in a barely 'shivering' liquid. What's more, our hostess knew how to cook. She just could not see what was happening in the fish kettle!

If you have a home with a big larder and walk-in cupboards, these will profit by having their own light. As one often enters these with both hands full, the best method of switching the light on and off is by a door latch switch. As the light is automatically cut out when the door is closed, in exactly the same way as in self-illuminated refrigerators, you do not run any risk of wasting electricity.

It really is false economy to skimp on lighting in the kitchen, and the same applies to socket outlets. There were two in my kitchen when I moved in, both in fairly inaccessible places. One was in a narrow space between the built-in cupboard and the cooker. It was just too high for comfortable reaching and, whenever I rushed to it with my customary energy, I either grazed my knuckles or broke a nail.

I love cooking and I am very good at clearing up as I go. I can produce a four- or five-course meal for a dozen people without leaving a trace in the kitchen of any work having been done, except a blend of delicious smells. It is one of my vanities to do all the work myself, but I do not want the state of my manicure to betray this, so I declared socket No. 1 unusable.

The second socket, unbelievably, was by the side of the refrigerator, almost at floor level. I used that one only once, for when I straightened up again, the massive understructure of the mantlepiece tried its best to knock me out.

I like a selection of double and single sockets above each working surface. My general advice would be: decide how many socket outlets you need, add a couple for good measure, work out where you want them, then get professional help. As the use of electrical appliances in the kitchen increases a separate ring circuit may be required to provide sufficient outlets. *Any rewiring should be entrusted only to qualified professionals.* Local Electricity Board showrooms supply lists of members of the National Inspection Council for Electrical Installation Contracting.

ELECTRICAL APPLIANCES

Now for a few items of equipment which I think deserve special mention.

Carving knife

I find my electric carving knife a great drudge remover. It has two blades with serrated hardened edges moving rapidly side by side when the control button is pushed. Immediately the finger is taken off, the motor stops. To use the knife you just guide it through the food; sawing or downward pressure is not needed and most things, including fresh baked bread, cakes, stacks of sandwiches, fruit, and vegetables can be cut easily and quickly with a downward movement. Apart from being able to slice foodstuffs as thinly or as thickly as required in a relatively short time, it has the additional advantage of getting more out of the Sunday joint and turning the user into an expert carver.

There are two types of electric carving knives: the mains models which plug into the socket and the chargeable cordless type. The cordless type is heavier but needs no flex. It has a stand which is plugged into the mains supply and, when the slicer is in its stored position on the stand, the battery is recharged. For convenience – and so it is ready for everyday use – an electric carving knife should be kept in or on its stand on a work top or it should be mounted on the wall.

Can opener

If there is one gadget which is more likely to cause an accident than a blunt knife, it is a blunt, bent can opener.

An electric can opener is simple to operate. It has a cutting wheel and there is a magnet to hold the can and lid. The can is held against the cutting wheel and the lever pulled over to grip the can edge. Usually a button is pressed and this starts the motor to drive the cutter round the edge of the can. The operation is quick and easy whatever the shape of the can.

Knife sharpener

Electric knife sharpeners are very similar in appearance to the manual type and most have the extra facility of being able to sharpen scissors and small woodworking chisels. Skill is usually required in sharpening knives manually but electric sharpeners are so designed that the knife is put in at the correct angle and pulled against the rotating grinding wheels, producing a very fine edge. Knives should be sharpened regularly, for it is a fact that blunt knives cause more accidents than sharp ones.

Vegetable peelers

These can be purchased as a separate item or as an attachment to some food mixers. They work by tumbling the vegetables in water over an abrasive disc. As the vegetables are thrown around the skin is removed. Some models claim to peel 4 lb (2 kg) of potatoes in 1 minute. If this claim is correct, a vegetable peeler could be a boon to a family that goes in for potato eating in a big way.

Waste disposer

It is estimated that every one of us is responsible each day for producing 2 lb (1 kg) of food and kitchen waste. A sobering thought. How do we get rid of it? The most hygienic way of disposing of kitchen scraps is through an electric waste-disposal unit fitted into the sink.

If you have a waste disposer, then, almost all the remaining household refuse will be the kind that offers no real health risk: dry goods, plastic wrappings, cans and bottles, and packets.

A waste disposer grinds up all the food waste into tiny scraps to flush away down the drain. Some manufacturers have a scheme whereby their waste disposers are fitted by their own installers for a standard fee. Choose a waste disposer that carries the BEAB label to show it has been tested for electrical safety.

COOKERS

ELECTRIC COOKERS

If the kitchen is the most important room in the house, the cooker is the most important piece of equipment. What should you buy? The choice is vast and tantalizing. It would be marvellous to have one of those elegant black and steel 'stay-clean' cookers with two independent autotimed ovens, a grill, and a rotisserie. You could roast at high temperature in one oven and, at the same time, slow bake in the other. But if you are destined to do your cooking in a mini-kitchenette, then one of those split-level very small cookers might be the better solution.

If you are planning to buy, let me impress on you the wisdom of visiting your local Electricity Board and asking to be shown the large range that is now available. Always read and follow the instructions supplied with every cooker. Particularly important are details of oven positions and the guide to temperature and cooking times. Modern electric cookers have quick-heating ovens and fast-boiling rings: they cook silently and efficiently but the greatest and most labour-saving advantage of electric cooking is undoubtedly its cleanliness. Electric cooking is flameless. The elements give off nothing but heat. All of this helps the kitchen stay clean and fresh.

The standard electric cooker has four boiling rings set into a hob and it has a grill and an oven. On some cookers the grill chamber serves as a second oven. There is also a smaller version with a grill, a good-sized oven, and two, three, or four boiling rings.

The usual size of electric boiling rings is 7 in. (about 18 cm) in diameter. Some cookers have all rings the same size; others have two different-sized rings with varying heat outputs. The dual ring has a switch to turn on the whole ring or (for heating small pans) the centre portion only.

From a gentle simmer to the fastest boil, with every possible setting in between – modern electric rings have infinitely variable control. Heat at every setting is absolutely constant, and unaffected by draughts. Control knobs vary the heat up and down like a tap, and many have visual indicators to show which rings are in use and their setting.

Some electric cookers have a special thermostatic 'pan-sensing' device on one of the rings. With this, the normal control knob can be adjusted to prevent liquids boiling over, for simmering, and for holding deep fat at a safe temperature.

AUTOMATIC COOKERS

Don't be afraid of your automatic cooker – it is just another piece of equipment designed to serve you. With a bit of sensible planning, it's as good as having a magic wand, except that you will still have the satisfaction of having produced the meal yourself.

The advantages of these easy, practical, and time- and labour-saving cookers are obvious.

Say you have guests coming to dinner and you know you will get home from work an hour before they are due. With good use of your automatic cooker, you can have half an hour to bath and change and half an hour to lay the table and put on fresh vegetables to cook. The rest of your meal will be ready. Impossible? Not at all and I hope to convince you by the time you have read this chapter. I often entertain on working days and seldom have more than half an hour at home before my guests arrive. Nor does your menu need to bring back echoes of boarding-school meals. Let no one tell you that an automatic cooker is useful only for stews and milk puddings. On the contrary, you can enhance your reputation as a clever hostess.

Decide on your main course and assemble it ready for the oven. Then choose one of the hors d'œuvres and a cold sweet, which can be prepared a day in advance, and leave in the refrigerator ready to serve.

You could, for example, start with taramasalata, pâté, or avocado with shellfish and have coq au vin or bœuf à la mode as a main course. With a simply dressed salad on the side and either with a good cheese or a fruit or liqueur mousse or ice as a dessert, you have a meal fit to set before anyone. Recipes for all the dishes mentioned are given in the book. Both coq au vin and bœuf à la mode are particularly suitable for automatic cooking, as are all casserole dishes and dishes requiring slow braising.

Are there people in your household who have to get up at crack of dawn and like a hot breakfast? Entrust it to your automatic oven overnight and it will be ready in the morning.

I think entertaining friends at home is one of the joys of living, and I am all for any device which will make the job easier and saves me time and my guests the embarrassment of seeing me working my fingers to the bone, rushing around heaving pots and pans, instead of being ready to join them in a drink. The autotimer is just the device which answers this purpose.

If you have a freezer and go in for batch baking, you will find the automatic oven a great boon – think of being able to go out and leave the last batch for the oven to finish off. And it switches itself off when the job is done!

Are you planning a big Christmas lunch or some other family reunion? You can put a turkey or a Sunday joint in the oven, set the timer, and be free to go out or do a hundred and one other things you may want to do.

You can put a complete meal in the cold oven and have it waiting for you when you return home. For this you need to choose compatible oven companions – dishes which can be cooked at approximately the same temperature and for about the same length of time. You won't spoil anything if one of the dishes is cooked for 10–15 minutes longer or at a slightly higher or lower temperature.

In calculating cooking time for a complete meal, always take the time required for cooking the dish which takes the longest, choose vegetables which are suitable for the meal, and remember that their size has a bearing on the cooking time required. If you are roasting a large joint, choose large potatoes and leave them whole. To accompany a small joint, use smaller potatoes, or cut large ones into quarters.

You can further adjust cooking time by reversing positions of dishes in the oven, or wrapping food in foil. To shorten cooking time, use enamel dishes, which heat quicker than earthenware. To lengthen cooking time, cover a dish with aluminium foil. Brush potatoes with oil or melted fat and put in a roasting tin. You can also use carrots, parsnips, onions, leeks, celery, and whole tomatoes. Some frozen vegetables, such as sweet corn, mixed vegetables, etc., can be quite successful; put them, frozen, into the oven in a covered dish, with a little butter, salt, and water. In fact, a great many dishes of all categories are suitable for automatic cooking: roast meat and poultry, casseroles of all kinds, baked fish, meat or fish pies, soups, steamed and baked puddings, fruit charlottes and crumbles, stewed fruit. For steamed puddings, cover the basin well, stand it in a tin with water halfway up the pudding basin and bake in the centre of the oven. In short, any dish which can start from cold and be left in the oven until you are ready to serve, is suitable for automatic cooking.

Pie tops of flaky pastry and 'dry' flaky pastry preparations can be baked very successfully. Rich fruit cakes can be baked overnight.

Only two categories are *not* suitable for automatic oven cooking:

1. Puff pastry preparations and pastry dishes with liquid in the filling, because puff pastry must go from a refrigerator into a hot oven and liquid in the filling causes the bottom layer of the pastry to become soggy.

2. Anything which needs less than about 30 minutes to cook, e.g. Swiss rolls, Victoria sandwich cakes, etc.

The instructions which come with your cooker will explain in detail exactly how it works. The basic operation is very simple.

1. Make sure the main switch is on.
2. Set correct oven temperature.
3. Check that the clock shows the right time.
4. Set the starting and finishing times.
5. Put the food in the oven.

When the cooking is completed, remember to return the control to 'manual' setting. If you neglect to do so, the oven will not switch on next time you need it for ordinary cooking.

To make efficient use of your automatic cooker, get to know it well. Study the manufacturer's instructions as you would the manual of your new car. Once you know your cooker's characteristics, you need not fear anything 'going wrong'. You can rely on it to help you produce delicious meals with the minimum of time and effort.

As for any successful production, have a couple of 'rehearsals'. Cook a few dishes while you observe how the automatic controls function. Set the oven to start an hour or so in advance and for a trial run of 45–50 minutes. See the oven turn itself on and off and you can't fail to acquire complete confidence in your cooker.

The autotimer
The autotimer works in conjunction with a 12-hour electric clock which is built into the control panel. This enables you to set the oven to turn itself on and off at selected times within the period of 12 hours, ahead of the setting time. It cannot be set to start more than 12 hours ahead. It can be set to start at any time within the 12-hour span, but should you wish to start a dish just at the end of the 12 hours, delay time, it can be finished with controls returned to 'manual' or 'normal' setting.

You can safely let your autotimer look after your cooking when you are otherwise engaged. Simply set the starting time, finishing time, and oven temperature – and the rest is done for you. One word of caution: do not leave highly perishable food, such as raw meat or fish, in the oven for too long on a hot, humid day.

Split level cookers offer great flexibility in kitchen planning. They are much more convenient. For one thing, you don't need to bend to use the oven.

They provide a choice of grill positions. You can have it above or below the oven. The oven/grill and the hob are separate units. They can be built in as required for the most advantageous working layout.

The hob can be fitted into a different part of the kitchen. Alternatively, you could incorporate separate electric boiling discs in a split-level arrangement, instead of a hob unit. These discs can be housed in any non-flammable material to suit your needs: stainless steel, stone, slate, marble, etc.

You can have the discs arranged in any way you like, provided you leave a space of 6 in. (15 cm) between them. With the exception of individual discs, all the controls for the split-level hob are usually on the hob, rather than on the front. This puts them out of reach of small children and therefore makes them that much safer.

All makers of kitchen fitments make specially designed units for housing these cookers. This does away with the uninspiring white-box appearance of some cookers and gives one an opportunity of establishing the style and preserving the colour scheme of one's kitchen.

The cabinet for housing the split-level oven must provide for adequate ventilation, as otherwise it could lead to a fire hazard. When mounted, the oven must be absolutely level, to enable you to close the doors properly. Split-level units can be supplied with left- or right-hand opening doors, to make it more convenient to set down dishes.

Some ovens are fitted with rotating spits, and have black glass panels which enable you to see how the cooking progresses. Some have gauze grease traps which can be easily removed for washing. All you need do is rinse the gauze trap in the sink. Even better, some new split-level cookers have a choice of hobs and ovens that will not get dirty or will clean themselves.

It is not necessary to have a cooker hood with a split-level oven. The extractor fan can easily cope with whatever steam has to be extracted.

SPLIT-LEVEL COOKERS

DOUBLE-WIDTH COOKERS

Double-width cookers have four boiling rings and plenty of hob space for resting pans; they provide extra capacity with two large ovens, side by side. The grill is either in one of the ovens or in a separate compartment. One of the new double-width cookers has a high-level grill and a solid, non-stick griddle on the hob. There is also a separate plate-warming drawer.

MINI-COOKERS

The mini-cooker is becoming increasingly popular because of its versatility. Originally it was designed for use in holiday cottages or bed-sitting rooms, but more and more it is being used in flatlets, by elderly people, or as a secondary cooker in large family homes. This type of cooker can be set at any height, and is particularly suitable for disabled people, especially those confined to a wheelchair. It has two boiling rings, an oven, and a grill, and is capable of cooking a meal for up to three or four people. There is also a split-level model of this small cooker.

NEW COOKERS

Some new cookers now have a 'fan-oven'.

The oven has one circular element surrounding a small fan behind the back panel. Fan and element work together and heated air flows round the oven instead of relying on convection, so the whole oven heats up more quickly and stays at a very even temperature. This method provides twice the shelf space with even browning on every shelf. Further advantages are less shrinkage of joints of meat, reduced cooking cost, and a cleaner oven.

These fan-assisted ovens are particularly recommended for freezer enthusiasts. Their temperatures are so even that you need never worry about the shelf on which you place your baking tins. You can fill the oven to capacity; three and even four shelves can be used. Batch bake in quantity, use what you need, and freeze the rest.

Because 'Stay-Clean' now works at a lower temperature, which makes it more efficient, it is used for lining fan ovens. The new full-size oven is fitted with an interior light and both the fan and the oven element are fully autotimed.

Heat recovery in fan ovens is so fast that there is no need for an inner glass door. When the door is open the fan and element are automatically switched off.

There are cookers with ceramic hobs. These are

made of very tough, heat-resisting opaque glass, and the completely flat, smooth surface has the electric heating elements concealed on the underside. The outside edges of any ceramic top are sealed to prevent liquids penetrating inside or underneath, and the hob is easily wiped clean. One of the main advantages is that the ordinary surface of the hob, when not actually cooking, makes a good work surface.

Among the new models there are built-in ovens in attractive colours with every refinement. I must confess, one particular feature of the new cookers has great appeal to me. It is the fact that they clean themselves. Theoretically, because all ovens are coated with a vitreous enamel, keeping them clean should present no difficulty. All one has to do is wipe them with a damp cloth after use. Yet it is incredible how quickly the ovens of even fastidious cooks get dirty, and there are few more repulsive jobs than having to clean a really neglected oven. There is a whole range of ovens, including built-in models, which make this unpleasant chore unnecessary.

The 'Self-Cleaning' method reduces even the heaviest baked-on spill-overs to a fine odourless white ash which can be wiped away in seconds. This cleaning cycle takes about 2 hours and needs to be carried out about twice a month.

The process involves heating the locked oven to about 900 °F (450 °C) which causes the splashes and spills to be carbonized. When the temperature is lowered to about 500 °F (250 °C) the oven looks as immaculate as the day it was installed. Glass doors are not usually fitted to self-clean ovens, but there is a model with a window, which during the self-cleaning cycle is protected by a special metal shield.

This method is very efficient, but one would not resort to it more often than once in 2 or 3 weeks.

The latest development is the 'Stay-Clean' method. The walls and roof of the oven are coated with a special form of vitreous enamel, which combines with heat and oxygen and vaporizes splashes of fat during the cooking before they can bake on. In some models, each time the oven reaches baking temperature, stains from grease splashes and other light oven soiling begin to disperse and are soon eliminated.

ROTISSERIE

A rotisserie can be a very useful adjunct in a kitchen. It provides an extra grill, oven or plate warmer, but its main purpose is to spit-roast food. Most models have kebab attachments, which are excellent for all dishes cooked on skewers.

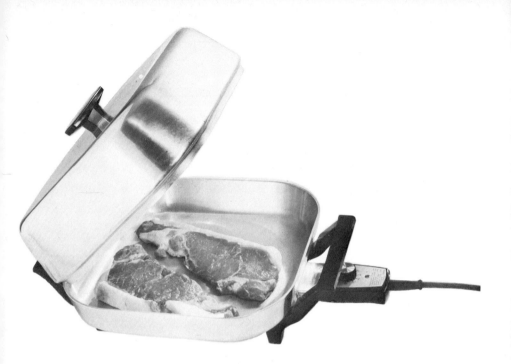

MULTI-COOKERS AND VERTICAL GRILLERS

In these days of kitchenettes no larger than a cupboard, space is so often a critical problem. In some cases, particularly where the owner has a penchant for quick and easy cooking, a full-sized cooker might find it difficult to earn its keep in terms of the space it takes up. Why not substitute appliances which can be stowed away and used as the occasion demands?

Among equipment of this type is a multi-cooker which occupies less than $1\frac{1}{2}$ square feet (1250 square centimetres) of table or shelf space and which is as portable as a large casserole. This will boil, steam, fry, and roast a 6 lb (3 kg) joint, or even two chickens of 3 lb each.

For grilling enthusiasts, a very small amount of space will accommodate a vertical griller and toaster that will grill meat and vegetables on one side while it toasts on the other.

Electric mixers come in various models and sizes, elaborate and simple, expensive and reasonable. There are hand-held mixers and mixers with their own bowl and stand. A food mixer should be designed to keep speed reasonably constant, even if the load on the motor varies during mixing. Some beaters on cheaper hand models have been known to bend or break, while some motors are not strong enough to take attachments or deal with coarse ingredients or heavy mixtures. As with all electrical equipment, always buy a mixer that carries the BEAB label to show that it has been tested for electrical safety.

The instruction book which explains a particular model should be read through first, because even experienced cooks will find helpful tips there.

Take note of how to clean the mixer: it should always be disconnected, and the motor body should never be immersed in water. Wiping with a dry or slightly damp cloth is all that is needed. Some sticky mixtures splash the body of the motor; the splashes should be wiped off as soon as possible after use.

A mixer basically does the work of a hand whisk or wooden spoon, with the blades or whisks moving at a fairly high speed to do the stirring more quickly and efficiently. Its capacity should never be exceeded because putting too much food into the bowl causes undue strain on the motor. Running the motor too long at a time is also detrimental: 5 or 6 minutes is the recommended limit. If more mixing is needed, the motor should be switched off and rested for about 5 minutes.

With a multispeed mixer, the speed used will vary with the kind of food being mixed. In general, the slow speed is for beginning operations such as mixing egg yolks and seasonings for mayonnaise; for mixing packet soups; or for creaming potatoes. The speed is gradually increased for these. The higher speed is for creaming fats and making smooth batters. The fastest speed beats air into egg whites and cream to lighten them. The speeds can be changed without switching off.

An electric mixer is often used to cream fat and sugar. It is easier if the fat is not too cold and firm, so avoid taking it straight from the refrigerator. Otherwise, warm the mixing bowl first.

The bladed beaters or whisks are to beat air into food such as egg whites as well as to emulsify ingredients as in mayonnaise, or simply for beating whole eggs for omelettes and other dishes. The spiral hooks are for kneading heavier mixtures such as fruit cake and pastry, and for yeast doughs.

A mixer with a bowl and stand of its own is really labour-saving because you can leave it to get on with the beating while you do something else. If a mixture builds up on the sides, scrape it down into the bowl with a plastic or rubber spatula – but switch off the motor before doing so. When making mayonnaise or beating egg whites, keep the blades in the centre. For other mixtures it is better to move the beaters around the bowl.

An advantage of a model which can be removed from its stand or an independent hand one is that it can be used wherever needed. If there is a socket outlet near the stove you may like to use it there.

Hand-held mixers can be used for creaming fat and sugar, making light cake mixes, whisking egg whites, rubbing fat into flour, and all the general kitchen cooking jobs. The better ones have three speeds which enables one to have a speed slow enough to fold in flour, but fast enough to beat a batter, and some models have 'electronic' controls, where the mixer itself adjusts its speed to the mixture being made. With a number of hand-held mixers a small blender attachment or coffee mill can be fitted, but the quantity that can be made with a hand-held machine is less than that which would be obtained with a large table model.

Many hand-held models can be fitted to a stand so that mixing can be carried out with minimum attention. A good stand/bowl attachment to hand mixers should turn and revolve to get every part of the mixture mixed. The table models usually take many more attachments such as a blender/liquidizer, a coffee grinder or coffee mill, a mincer, a juice extractor, plus many more including even a sausage maker and a potato peeler. But they need a stronger motor which adds to the cost.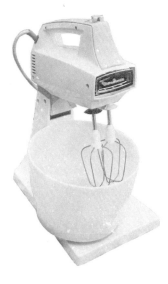

A good mixer should be able to rub in, stir, whisk, whip, knead, and beat. These operations are not identical. Rubbing-in is a smooth, fast, rubbing action, mixing fat with flour, breaking it up and lifting in the mixture to let in air. Stirring is a slower action; you stir round and round horizontally for batter and mayonnaise for instance. Whisking means using the food mixer at its fastest speed, as when whisking egg whites or meringues or a fatless sponge. Whipping is a similar action but applied to thicker and heavier mixtures and often at a medium speed. Kneading needs a special beater – the dough hook – as it is a downward, pounding and lifting action with weight behind it. Some makers supply different beater attachments to suit the ingredients, while some design the beaters and bowls to suit all the actions, but place the emphasis on using the correct speed and adding in some other ingredients gradually during the mixing. This is why, I repeat, it pays to read the manufacturer's instruction booklet to get the best results.

In most recipes for cakes, puddings, and sweets, the lightness of the texture depends on the amount of air that is beaten into the ingredients. An electric beater not only makes preparation quicker and easier but also gives better results than hand mixing.

One job for which a mixer is invaluable is the beating of egg whites until stiff for meringues, soufflés,

and many other dishes. To ensure success every time, use egg whites that are at least 24 hours old, and make sure that the bowl in which they are beaten and the beaters themselves are scrupulously clean and dry. Even a trace of yolk will prevent the whites beating up properly. If eggs are usually kept in the refrigerator, allow them to reach room temperature before whisking. Use a high speed, but, if soft peaks only are wanted, switch off after a few seconds.

Thorough whisking is the secret of light ice-cream. If the mixture is light and fluffy before it is frozen, the texture will be greatly improved and it will be much nicer to eat than if it is too solid.

When it comes to cake making, a mixer is particularly useful. Whether the recipe calls for an initial creaming of fat and sugar or whisking of eggs and sugar, you will get more volume and therefore a lighter result with electric beaters. Warming the bowl and the beaters slightly before putting in the fat makes creaming easier.

To warm the bowl and the beaters, plunge into hot, *not boiling*, water then drain and dry thoroughly. This will speed up your mixing operation and also prevent creamed mixture climbing and sticking to the beaters or the side of the bowl. If your mixer has a choice of bowl size, or if it is a hand-held machine, choose the bowl size most suitable for the amount of mixture you are using. If using the whisking method, remember to have the eggs at room temperature. Always use castor sugar and make sure that the flour is sieved and dry before folding it in gently.

Bowls and beaters are designed for even mixing, but if the mixture sticks to the side of the bowl, then, as I have said, stop the machine and scrape it down with a spatula. Check that the beaters are straight and correctly fitted into their sleeve and check the manufacturer's instructions to ensure you are using the right speed. On a table model use only the manufacturer's bowl and stand. Replace damaged, badly bent beaters.

Remember the food mixer can do its job much more quickly than someone mixing by hand; cream will turn to butter if it is beaten too long, pastry becomes difficult to handle if rubbing-in is carried on for too long or if you use too much fat. How long is too long is difficult to say – only experience will tell you, but do read the manufacturer's instruction book. The machine works faster than you, so control the speed and never try to rush things by turning up to the maximum setting every time. General rules: the lighter the mixture the higher the speed required to do the job properly; the smaller the quantity the lower the speed is required.

A large Christmas, birthday, or wedding cake can be a great chore. This is where an efficient mixer comes into its own, but it can only operate as you direct it. If a cake is 'heavy' you may have mixed the flour in too vigorously or for too long. The lower speed is used for folding in the flour and the machine should be switched off as soon as the flour is incorporated.

Some icings present certain difficulties. I often wished I were one of those Oriental goddesses – for no other reason than the number of arms they possess. It would be useful to have one hand for holding a bowl, a second for beating egg whites, and a third for pouring on syrup, when these jobs have all to be done at the same time. Mixers can cope with this satisfactorily.

Fudges and home-made sweets can also be made in the mixer. Remember not to overload its capacity, because some of these mixtures are fairly heavy and may put too much strain on the motor.

Juice extractors and separators can be obtained as a separate unit or sometimes as an attachment to the large food-mixer/food-preparation machines. A juice extractor has a rotating cone and strainer to remove juice from citrus fruits. You press the halved oranges, grapefruit or lemons by hand, but with an electrically operated extractor, the job is quicker and easier and you get more juice from the fruit. Juice separators extract juice from fruit or vegetables, separate the fleshy part, and strain off the juice. These are very useful in home wine making.

Recipes for dishes of many categories which are easy to make with a mixer are now given. In addition, you can use both mixers and blenders for making your own skin care and other beauty preparations, as well as papier-mâché toys.

JUICE EXTRACTORS AND SEPARATORS

Recipes using Mixers

Mayonnaise

Make sure your mixer bowl is dry and cool. Put in egg yolks, salt, pepper, mustard, and half the lemon juice. Start whisking on low speed. Drip in oil gradually, keeping the speed slow, until the mayonnaise thickens. Whisk in the remainder of the lemon juice.

Mayonnaise can also, of course, easily be made in the blender. Follow the same recipe and the manufacturer's instructions.

2 raw egg yolks
salt and pepper
3–4 tablespoons lemon juice (or vinegar)
pinch dry mustard
½ pint (250 ml) olive oil

Cheese, Onion, and Bacon Tart

Put the flour and salt in the mixer bowl, add butter, fat, and cut into pieces. Using dough hooks at speed 1, mix in the fat until it resembles fine breadcrumbs. Add the water and continue at speed 1 until the pastry forms a ball. Roll out and use to line a 10 in. (25 cm) fluted flan tin.

Fry bacon and onions until tender, and place in flan tin. Grate cheese and spread over filling. Whisk eggs with beaters at speed 1, add cream, and pour mixture over flan.

Cook at 400 °F (200 °C) until the custard is set and golden brown on top.

6 Servings
6 oz (150 grams) plain flour
pinch of salt
2 oz (50 g) butter
1 oz (25 g) white fat
2–3 tablespoons cold water
8 oz (200 g) chopped lean bacon
2 large chopped onions
8 oz (200 g) Gruyère cheese
3 eggs
medium carton double cream

Short Crust Pastry

Use the mixer for all short crust pastry, i.e. when the fat has to be rubbed into the flour. Here is a general short crust pastry recipe for savoury dishes.

Put flour, salt, and butter into mixer bowl. Set to lowest possible speed and mix until the fat and the flour have been thoroughly amalgamated. Switch off, stir in enough water to bind, and – using a knife – mix to a stiff paste.

8 oz (200 g) plain flour
pinch salt
4 oz (100 g) butter or other fat, cut in small pieces
iced water

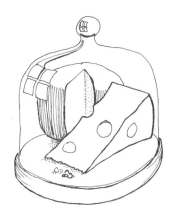

Sweet Short Crust Pastry

Proceed as above but use only butter or margarine, add sugar to taste – anything from 2 to 4 tablespoons for the quantity of flour given above – and use a mixture of beaten egg and iced water to bind the pastry.

Sponge Cake

In cake making, the mixer is very useful for sponge mixtures, for whisking eggs and sugar, for creaming fat and sugar, for beating egg whites, for meringue mixtures, for yeast dough. You can therefore adapt recipes given in other sections of this book for use with a mixer. Check setting of speeds for various operations in the manufacturer's instructions.

3 eggs
3 oz (75 g) sugar
3 oz (75 g) sifted self-raising flour
2 oz (50 g) melted butter

Pre-heat oven to 350 °F (180 °C). Grease and flour a 7 in. (18 cm) cake tin.

Use a large mixing bowl. Put eggs and sugar into it, switch on, and whisk until thick. Fold in flour, then add butter, which must be lukewarm. Make sure it is well blended in.

Spoon mixture into cake tin, bake for 25–30 minutes. To test for readiness, without removing the cake from oven, press gently with finger. If the cake bears no sign of the imprint, it is ready. Leave for a few minutes to cool in the tin, then turn out on to a cake rack.

Serve plain, or iced, or split and sandwiched with jam and cream.

12 oz (300 g) self-raising flour
½ level teaspoon salt
2 oz (50 g) margarine or butter
3 oz (75 g) castor sugar
6 tablespoons chopped walnuts
2 oz (50 g) candied orange peel
2 beaten eggs
½ pint (250 ml) milk

Nut and Orange Loaf

Sift flour and salt into a bowl, rub in butter or margarine, add sugar, chopped walnuts, and chopped candied peel. Mix to a soft dough with the beaten eggs and milk, using the dough hooks at speed 2. Turn into a greased 2 lb (1 kg) loaf tin, decorate with halved walnuts, and cook at 375 °F (190 °C) for 1 hour.

6 oz (150 g) margarine
6 oz (150 g) castor sugar
3 medium eggs
6 oz (150 g) self-raising flour
a little raspberry jam

Victoria Sandwich

Using the beaters, cream the softened fat in the mixer bowl at speed 1 for about a minute, then add the sugar, increase to speed 2 and beat until fluffy and pale in colour. Add the eggs one at a time at speed 1.

When they are well mixed in, change to the dough hooks and beat in the flour at speed 1, adding a little milk, if necessary, to make a soft consistency.

Do not overbeat after adding the flour, but switch off as soon as it is all incorporated. Turn into well-floured sandwich tins, cook for 20 minutes at 375 °F (190 °C). When cool, sandwich together with raspberry jam and sprinkle with castor sugar.

Devil's Food Cake

Sift flour, salt, soda, and cocoa twice. Soften margarine, add sugar 3 oz (75 g) at a time. Melt chocolate and milk in a basin over hot water, add the egg yolks to this, and allow to cool. Add to the sugar and butter, mix in the flour, and fold in egg whites which have been whisked with the beaters at speed 3 until stiff. Turn into two well-greased 8 in. (20 cm) sandwich tins. Cook at 400 °F (200 °C) 20–25 minutes.

8 oz (200 g) self-raising flour
pinch of salt
pinch of bicarbonate of soda
2 teaspoons cocoa
5 oz (125 g) margarine or butter
6 oz (150 g) sugar
4 oz (100 g) plain chocolate
4 tablespoons milk
2 large or 3 small eggs, separated
toasted split almonds

Chocolate Butter Icing

For the butter icing, put the butter into the bowl and cream with the beaters at speed 1. When soft add sugar gradually, still at speed 1. Lastly add the cooled melted chocolate. Sandwich the cake together with the icing when cool, and spread the remaining icing on top and round the sides. Brown the almonds under the grill and roll the sides of the cake in them. Use any remaining almonds to decorate the top of the cake.

3 oz (75 g) unsalted butter
6 oz (150 g) sifted icing sugar
2 oz (50 g) plain chocolate melted in 2
* tablespoons water*

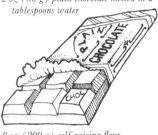

Scones

Place the flour and the fat cut into pieces in the mixer bowl and, using the hooks at speed 1, mix until the texture is that of fine breadcrumbs. Add the sugar, continue mixing for a further few minutes, then add the milk and mix at speed 1 until it makes a soft dough. Turn on to a floured board and knead well.

Roll out to ½ in. (1 cm) thickness and, using a cutter make into rounds. Place on a greased baking tray, glaze with beaten egg. Cook at 450 °F (230 °C) for about 15 minutes.

8 oz (200 g) self-raising flour
2 oz (50 g) margarine or butter
2 oz (50 g) castor sugar
¼ pint (250 ml) milk
beaten egg to glaze

Brandy Snaps

Warm margarine, syrup, and sugar until melted. Add flour and ginger and mix well. Place teaspoons of the mixture on a well-greased tray, leaving a good space between each spoonful as the mixture spreads. Cook in a moderate oven at 350 °F (180 °C) for about 10 minutes, or until the mixture is golden brown.

Allow them to cool a little before removing from tray and rolling round the handle of a wooden spoon. When cold fill with double cream, whipped with the beaters at speed 1 until thick, and sprinkle with pistachio nuts.

2 oz (50 g) margarine
2 oz (50 g) golden syrup
2 oz (50 g) sugar
2 oz (50 g) flour
¼ teaspoon ground ginger
double cream
chopped pistachio nuts

Strawberry Fluff

4 Servings
1 lb (½ kg) hulled strawberries
1 oz (25 g) castor sugar
2 egg whites

Purée the strawberries with sugar to taste in a blender. In a mixer, whisk the egg whites until very stiff, incorporating 2 tablespoons of castor sugar at the last stage of whisking. Fold the strawberry purée into the egg whites, spoon into serving goblets and keep cold until ready to serve.

Chocolate Mousse

4 Servings
4 oz (100 g) plain chocolate
1½ tablespoons sugar
2 raw yolks
2 tablespoons double cream
2 stiffly beaten egg whites
hazelnut biscuits (p. 183)

Put the chocolate through a grater. Combine chocolate, sugar, and yolks in a bowl over a pan of hot water and whisk until smooth.

Allow to cool, mix in cream, leave to cool immediately, then fold chocolate mixture into stiffly beaten egg whites. Pour into glasses, chill, and serve with hazelnut biscuits.

Lemon Mousse

6 Servings
3 egg yolks
6 oz (150 g) castor sugar
rind and juice of 3 small lemons
small packet of gelatine
¼ gill (60 ml) hot water
4 oz (100 ml) each double and single cream
3 egg whites
chopped toasted nuts to decorate

Put a lightly oiled collar round a soufflé dish of 1 pint or ½ litre capacity. Keep it in place with string and a paper-clip where the edges overlap. Put egg yolks, sugar, and rind and juice of the lemons into a large pudding basin. Stand it over a pan of simmering water and whisk, with a rotary beater, for 5 minutes. Take the basin from the pan, stand it on the table, and whisk for another 5 minutes.

Dissolve gelatine in the hot, but not boiling water; beat it into the egg and lemon mixture.

Beat the two creams together until they are thick, and stir them into the mixture.

Whisk the egg whites stiff, and fold them in carefully.

Leave to thicken for about 20 minutes, then pour into the soufflé dish. Cool, then put in refrigerator. Remove the collar when the soufflé has set, decorate with the chopped nuts. Serve chilled.

Maître d'Hôtel Butter

4 oz (100 g) butter
1 teaspoon salt
pinch black pepper
1½ tablespoons chopped parsley
1 tablespoon lemon juice

Cream the butter in a bowl with a mixer whisk, add salt, pepper, and parsley, mix well, blend in lemon juice little by little, and use as directed. Maître d'hôtel butter makes an excellent accompaniment for grilled meat or fish.

Orange Butter for Crêpes Suzette

Combine all ingredients in a mixing bowl; whisk until thoroughly mixed. Freeze in a rigid container. Thaw before use.

3 oz (75 g) unsalted butter
6–8 lumps orange sugar (see below)
2 tablespoons Grand Marnier or Curaçao

Orange or Lemon Sugar

To make orange or lemon sugar, rub the fruit with a sugar lump until it is completely covered with the rind. Scrape off and use this coloured surface. Repeat the operation until enough flavoured sugar is obtained.

Brandy Butter

With the mixer speed at medium, cream butter; sift in sugar, beating all the time until white and fluffy. Drip in brandy, mixing well. Spoon into a pretty serving dish. Chill well before serving.

8 oz (200 g) unsalted butter
8 oz (200 g) icing sugar
6 tablespoons brandy

This 'hard sauce', as the Americans call it, will keep for a fortnight in a covered jar in the refrigerator.

Rum Butter

As for brandy butter, substituting rum for brandy.

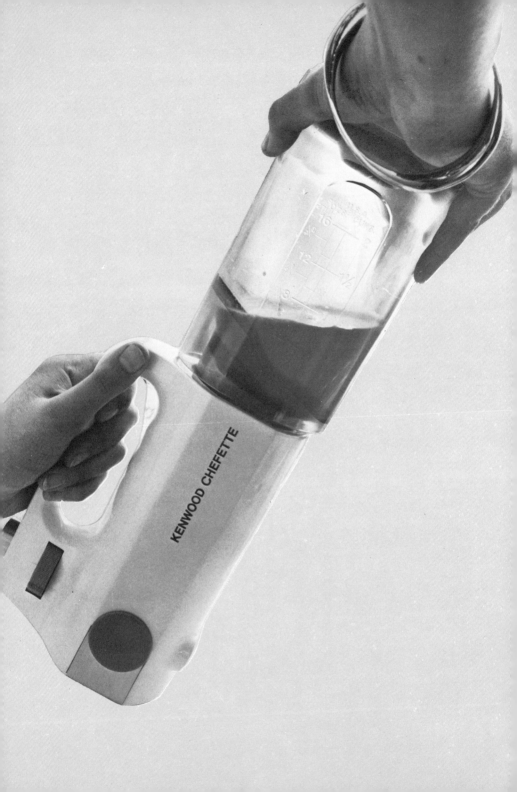

Blenders can be bought as a separate unit or as an attachment to a food mixer. They vary in size but usually will do the same job of work. However, the size chosen would be dependent upon the type of quantities that a user will require. In general, all blenders will chop, blend, liquidize, grind, pulp, and purée. The quickest and easiest way to get a smooth purée or to blend several ingredients together is with an electric blender. This can be used for fruits, vegetables, batters, dips, sauces, and dressings as well as for making delicious drinks and mayonnaise.

Once you have got into the habit of using one, it becomes very difficult to do without it – pressing a button is so much easier than sieving, straining or mixing by hand. When using a blender, it is important not to fill the goblet more than two-thirds full, because the contents will rise up when the power is switched on. There must be room for movement, especially in the case of very liquid mixtures like soups and drinks.

Never run the motor when the goblet is empty or if it contains dry ingredients only. Maximum running time is 45 seconds: if longer is needed, the appliance should be switched off, rested for a minute, and then rerun for another short session only.

Fix the goblet firmly down on to the motor base to ensure a perfect connection between the two parts and cover with the lid before switching on. The ingredients very soon emulsify into a smooth purée, so that small quantities of food for babies and items like mint sauce can be made very easily.

Vegetables should be cut into 1 in. cubes; citrus fruits quartered or cut up into smaller pieces; apples, pears, and other fruits need only be cored or stoned before they are roughly chopped for processing. A few seconds in the machine does the rest.

The blender is a boon for a family with a young baby. When babies first start taking solid food, the amount they can eat at any one time is quite small. It seems hardly worth all the sieving and washing up. With a blender you can save time and trouble by making larger quantities of puréed foods, storing them in the refrigerator or freezer.

It is equally useful in catering for the elderly who may have difficulty in chewing. Nourishing, easily digestible meals can be prepared for invalids, who may not feel like eating, in which case it is all the more important to tempt them with well-balanced meals. With the aid of a blender, in minutes you can make a

very smooth purée soup, concentrated fruit and vegetable drinks, light fluffy desserts.

A blender is indispensable in preparing liquid or
semi-solid diets and concentrated high-protein slim-
ming dishes. You can ensure variety, control ingredients, and reduce your carbohydrate intake – if
that happens to be temporarily your abomination –
by avoiding all starchy thickening of soups and sauces.

Blenders are enormously versatile. A blender will
make breadcrumbs, mayonnaise, chop nuts, parsley,
and ice, change granulated sugar into castor sugar, and
some will even make a sandwich cake. For those who
like to make cocktails, it is an ideal way for mixing both
alcoholic and non-alcoholic drinks. The drinks need
not involve much preparation or time, particularly if

you have an electric fruit squeezer as well as a blender.

The appliance is simple to use and the only job which one must do is roughly chop foodstuffs, such as carrots, oranges, potatoes, etc. Recipes for various delicious summer drinks are given.

Some blenders have a small cap in the lid and this can be removed when the motor is running, enabling ingredients to be added on to the cutting blades, as when making breadcrumbs or adding oil slowly for making mayonnaise.

Large and small blenders

Small blenders are available as attachments for the smaller mixers. They are used for blending, chopping, and beating. For larger quantities, divide the ingredients into small batches. Never try to fill above the level marked on the goblet and never use boiling liquid. If this is not observed it is possible for the lid to be pushed off the goblet and it could result in hot liquids being sprayed over the user. The larger blender not only mixes larger quantities, but can sometimes be used for such jobs as making a one-stage sandwich cake. You can also make butter in the blender from the top of the milk or from cream left in the refrigerator. One method is to blend up at top speed for about a minute, pour off the buttermilk, add clean cold water, and give it a few more seconds. Pour the water away, squeeze the butter to expel as much moisture as possible, add salt to taste.

After several years of heavy use the cutter blades will become rough. Take the blender in for servicing – a new set of cutters can easily be fitted.

Recipes using Blenders

Taramasalata

Skin the roe, put in a bowl, cover with 6 tablespoons oil. Leave to soften for a quarter of an hour. Cut the crusts of bread and soak them in water. Squeeze out all surplus water. Put roe and bread into a blender and start liquidizing. Little by little blend in lemon juice and oil, adding the oil a spoonful at a time. Season with pepper to taste, add onion, garlic, and parsley, and switch on blender. Emulsify until the mixture is smooth. Pack into suitable containers, smooth the top, seal, wrap in heavy foil, and freeze. Thaw at room temperature for 1½ hours and serve with melba toast.

12 Servings
1 lb (½ kg) smoked cod's roe
12 oz (300 ml) olive oil
4 oz (100 g) stale white bread
juice of 1½ lemons
freshly ground pepper
1–2 tablespoons finely grated onion
and/or 2–3 crushed cloves garlic
3 tablespoons chopped parsley

Avocado with Prawn or Crayfish Mousse

Cut the avocados in half, remove stone, sprinkle with lemon juice to prevent discoloration.

Combine prawns or crayfish with cream and mayonnaise in a blender. Season with salt. Switch on and blend until smooth. Taste for seasoning, add a dash of lemon juice, blend for another 20 seconds.

Pile the cream on avocado pears, sprinkle with cayenne pepper.

6 Servings
3 ripe avocado pears
lemon juice
6 tablespoons peeled, cooked prawns
or crayfish tails
6 tablespoons cream
4 tablespoons mayonnaise
salt and cayenne pepper

Liver Spread

Cut liver into pieces and put into a blender with the other ingredients. Run for a few seconds until smooth and store in a cool place.

8 oz (200 g) lambs' liver, fried
gently in 2 oz (50 g) butter until
tender
1 spring onion, chopped
salt and pepper
1 clove garlic (optional)
¼ pint (100 ml) tomato juice

Bacon Pâté

Fry or grill the bacon and put through a mincer. Fry onion in butter, add to bacon, with all the pan juices. Add parsley, season with pepper and mustard, and mix well.

If you prefer a very smooth mixture, put the lot through a blender.

Cool; put into foil dishes, smooth top, seal with heavy foil and freeze. Thaw at room temperature, turn out, cut into portions of required size, and serve with hot toast.

6–8 Servings
12 oz (300 g) bacon
1 medium-sized chopped onion
2 oz (50 g) butter
1 tablespoon chopped parsley
freshly grated pepper
1–2 teaspoons freshly made mustard
(optional)

Devilled Eggs

4 hard-boiled eggs, shelled
¼ teaspoon made mustard
1 tablespoon mayonnaise
few drops tabasco
2 tablespoons single cream
salt and pepper to taste
paprika
chopped parsley or small tin anchovy
 fillets
lettuce leaves

Cut the eggs in half lengthwise and remove yolks. Put the whites to one side. Put yolks into blender with mustard, mayonnaise, tabasco, and cream, add seasoning and switch on for a few seconds until well blended and smooth. Refill the egg whites with the mixture, piling it up well, sprinkle with paprika, decorate with chopped parsley or a small twist of anchovy fillet, and serve on a bed of lettuce leaves.

Lentil Soup

6 Servings
1 pint (½ litre) lentils
water
1 large grated onion
1 quart (1 litre) scalded milk
salt and pepper
3 tablespoons cream

Soak lentils overnight. Cook with onion in lightly salted water until tender. Then strain, purée in a blender, and dilute with milk, season to taste, remove from heat, stir in cream, and serve.

Green Pea Soup

6 Servings
1½ lb (750 g) fresh or frozen green
 peas
lightly salted water
1 quart (1 litre) scalded milk
salt and pepper
3 tablespoons cream

Cook the peas in minimum of salted boiling water until just tender. Strain and purée in a blender. Dilute with milk, reheat, season to taste, and, just before serving, blend in cream.

Cream of Mushroom Soup

4 Servings
12 oz (300 g) mushrooms
2 chopped onions
3 oz (75 g) butter
2 tablespoons flour
1 pint (½ litre) milk
salt and pepper
4 oz (100 ml) cream

Reserve 4 oz (100 g) mushroom caps, chop the rest. Fry chopped mushrooms and onion in half the butter and pass through a blender. Slice reserved mushroom caps and fry in remaining butter until soft. Sprinkle in flour, cook, stirring for 2 minutes, without allowing the mixture to brown. Dilute with milk, stirring it in a little at a time. Simmer for 5 minutes with stirring, add mushroom and onion purée, and season to taste. Remove from heat, blend in cream, and serve at once.

Bavarian Creamed Liver Soup

6 Servings
1 oz (25 g) butter
1 finely chopped onion
1 lb (½ kg) diced calf liver
1½ tablespoons flour
1 quart (1 litre) stock
salt and pepper
pinch mace
4 oz (100 g) sour cream

Heat butter in a saucepan and fry onion until soft. Add liver and brown. Sprinkle in flour, blend well, cook on low heat for 3–4 minutes. Little by little add stock. Season to taste with salt and pepper, add mace, and simmer for 30 minutes.

Drain the liver and pass through a blender. Return to soup, reheat. Stir and serve with a topping of sour cream.

Vichyssoise

Heat butter in a saucepan and lightly fry leeks and onion, stirring with a wooden spoon. Add potatoes and cook together for 2–3 minutes. Add stock and simmer for 40 minutes. Pass through a blender and allow to cool.

When cold, blend in cream, season to taste with salt, pepper, and nutmeg. Chill, serve cold sprinkled with chopped chives.

4–6 Servings
2 oz (50 g) unsalted butter
3–4 sliced leeks, white part only
1 onion sliced
5 medium-sized potatoes, peeled and sliced finely
1¼ quarts (1¼ litres) chicken stock
1 gill (100 ml) double cream
salt and pepper
pinch nutmeg
1–1¼ tablespoons chopped chives

Turkish Soup

Cut cucumber into bite-sized pieces, salt well, and refrigerate for 2 hours or more, then wash off salt. Blend yoghurt, cucumber, and garlic in a blender. Serve chilled with a sprinkling of mint on top.

4–5 Servings
half a cucumber
3 cartons natural yoghurt
1 clove garlic
chopped mint to garnish

Cream of Vegetable Soup

Chop the vegetables coarsely, then fry in a little cooking oil, taking care not to brown them. Season, add stock cube and water, and simmer until the vegetables are cooked. Put the resulting mixture through the blender a little at a time, stir in the cream, and garnish with the croûtons just before serving.

1 small cabbage
3 large sticks celery
2 medium onions
2 carrots
2 tomatoes
1 large potato
3 leeks
a little cooking oil
salt and pepper
1 stock cube
1¼ quarts (1¼ litres) water
3 tablespoons cream
croûtons

Baked Cod, Spanish Style

Heat oven to 350 °F (180 °C).

Put the fish steaks into a lightly buttered oven-proof dish, season to taste. Purée the tomatoes in a blender. Add onion, garlic, parsley, and oil. Switch on and blend until smooth and well amalgamated. Cover the fish with this dressing and bake for 25 minutes.

4 Servings
4 cod steaks
a little butter
salt and pepper
½ lb (200 g) skinned tomatoes
1 small onion
1 clove garlic
1 tablespoon chopped parsley
1 tablespoon olive oil.

Salmon Quiche

Prepare the pastry case as described.

Put bread through the blender to make fine crumbs. Spread breadcrumbs on a sheet and bake in the oven until crisp. Break up fish into pieces – do not mash. Put fish and breadcrumbs into pastry case. Put eggs and milk into blender, season to taste, blend to mix milk. Pour into pastry case and bake in the oven pre-heated to 375–400 °F (190–200 °C) until set. Serve hot or cold.

4 Servings
pastry case as for asparagus quiche (p. 175)
2 oz (50 g) bread
12 oz (300 g) cooked or tinned salmon
2 eggs
½ pint (250 ml) warm milk
salt and pepper

4 Servings
2 medium onions
1 green pepper
4 oz (100 g) sliced mushrooms
4 oz (100 g) brown breadcrumbs
6 oz (150 g) grated cheese
3 eggs beaten
1 oz (25 g) butter
seasoning to taste
1 tablespoon chopped parsley
tomato sauce

Mushroom Loaf

Mince onions and pepper coarsely in chopper or mincer, then gently fry together in butter until almost cooked. Add sliced mushrooms and cook for further 5 minutes. Remove from heat, add rest of the ingredients except for tomato sauce and using half of the cheese only. Mix thoroughly, using hand mixer with hooks at speed 1. Press mixture into a greased loaf tin, sprinkle with rest of cheese, and bake in a moderate oven at 375 °F (190 °C) for 45 minutes. Turn out on to a hot dish and serve with tomato sauce.

4 oz (100 g) cream cheese
2–3 tablespoons mayonnaise
1 tablespoon single cream
salt to taste
2 oz (50 g) walnuts
pineapple rings
halved pears or peaches (fresh or tinned)
paprika
lettuce leaves

Fruit Salad with Cheese and Walnut Filling

Put the cream cheese, mayonnaise, cream, paprika, and salt to taste into the goblet and blend until well mixed. Remove and add walnuts which have been pulverized in the grinder. Adjust seasoning and fill rings of pineapple and halved pears or peaches with the mixture. Sprinkle the filling with paprika and arrange the fruit on a bed of crisp lettuce.

4 cloves garlic
water
6 oz (150 g) butter

Garlic Butter

Boil garlic in just enough water to cover for 5 minutes. Drain, and purée in a blender adding butter little by little. Store in a jar with a well-fitting lid.

To freeze butter, roll into pats or stamp out into shape, pack in boxes with a piece of cellophane between layers, and freeze.

To serve, use straight out of freezer.

Kneaded Butter

Blend 4 oz (100 g) butter with 3 oz (75 g) flour, mix into a smooth paste, and use as a quick liaison to bind sauces.

You will only need a tablespoon at a time, but it is useful to make a larger amount, which can be kept in a refrigerator, ready for use whenever required. The blender allows you to make a very smooth paste, but if you attempt to make the quantity you need for one application, the small amount of ingredients will get lost in the blender blades.

French Dressing

Put all the ingredients into the blender, cover, and switch on for about 30 seconds until blended together.

2 tablespoons tarragon vinegar or lemon juice
6 tablespoons salad oil
salt
freshly ground black pepper
½ clove garlic, finely crushed
¼ teaspoon French mustard
small slice onion or spring onion (optional)

Pancake Batter made in a Blender

Put milk and egg into blender goblet. Sprinkle in salt, then add flour. Switch on at low speed, little by little increase to high, and blend until the batter is smooth.

½ pint (250 ml) milk
1 egg
pinch salt
4 oz (100 g) plain flour

Fondant Icing

Mix all ingredients in a blender until smooth.

8 oz (200 g) sifted confectioners' sugar
2 tablespoons milk
¼ teaspoon almond or vanilla extract

Apple Sauce

Peel apples, core, and slice. Simmer with sugar, butter, and 2–3 tablespoons water for a few minutes, until soft. Allow to cool, then put into warmed blender goblet, and switch on. Start on low speed and gradually bring up to high. Reheat for use.

If you wish to freeze apple sauce, cool very quickly, decant into a rigid container, seal, label, and freeze, as described.

1 lb (½ kg) apples
2 oz (50 g) sugar
2 tablespoons butter

Mint Sauce

It takes only a few seconds to make mint sauce in a blender.

Put all ingredients into the goblet and switch on the blender at high speed. Transfer to a sauce-boat and leave to stand for a quarter of an hour to settle.

4 Servings
4 tablespoons mint leaves
2 tablespoons sugar
3 tablespoons white wine vinegar

Parsley Sauce

Make the white sauce as described. As soon as it thickens, add parsley, cook for a couple of minutes, and remove from heat. Warm the blender goblet, put the sauce into it, switch on to high speed and blend until smooth.

white sauce (p. 178)
chopped parsley to taste

Zabaglione

4 Servings
4 egg yolks
4 teaspoons icing sugar
4 tablespoons Marsala

Put the egg yolks into a double saucepan with the icing sugar and Marsala and whisk with hand mixer at speed 3 over gentle, then moderate, heat for about 5 minutes, until the mixture is very thick. Pour into small individual goblets and serve at once, accompanied by sponge fingers or ratafia biscuits.

The recipes which follow give an idea of the wide variety of delicious drinks that can be made – and you might enjoy inventing your own. Ice cubes, by the way, should be crushed a little before putting them into the blender.

Tomato Cocktail

4 Servings
8 large tomatoes
2 tablespoons lemon juice
pinch brown sugar
pinch celery salt
pinch cayenne pepper
2–3 teaspoons Worcester sauce
2 tablespoons crushed ice
4 twists lemon peel

Choose ripe tomatoes, skin them, and discard seeds. Combine all ingredients in the blender. Blend at high speed until smooth. Decant into chilled glasses. Add a lemon twist to each and serve.

Tomato and Cucumber Cocktail

½ small cucumber, peeled
1 medium tin tomato juice
2 tablespoons lemon juice
½ teaspoon Worcester sauce
½ clove garlic, crushed
crushed ice

Cut up some of the cucumber and blend with the rest of the ingredients. Serve iced, garnished with slices of cucumber floating on the top.

Milk Shakes

Add chosen fruit to milk (fresh or drained tinned fruit may be used): the goblet should not be more than two-thirds full. Blend till light and fluffy then serve straight away. Suitable fruits include bananas (use half a sliced banana and a squeeze of lemon juice), raspberries, sliced strawberries, and other soft fruits. Add a scoop of the appropriately flavoured ice-cream for extra richness.

Banana Milk Shake

For each helping allow half a banana, ½ teaspoon lemon juice, ½ tumbler cold milk, and a tablespoon ice-cream. Combine all ingredients in a blender. Switch on, gradually increase speed to high, blend until frothy.

Strawberry (or Raspberry) Milk Shake

As above, substituting 2 tablespoons of strawberries for banana.

Iced Coffee

Blend all ingredients in the blender for a few seconds. Pour into glasses.

¼ pint (250 ml) cold milk
2 dessertspoons coffee essence (or 2 teaspoons instant coffee dissolved in boiling water, sweetened with demerara sugar)
1 scoop coffee or vanilla ice-cream

Iced Chocolate

Dissolve a tablespoonful of drinking chocolate in a little hot coffee or water: put into the blender with a glass of cold milk and scoop of chocolate ice-cream. Run for a few seconds. Serve topped with whipped cream and grated chocolate.

Egg-nog

Blend the egg, cold milk, castor sugar, and vanilla essence for about 30 seconds, or until light and fluffy. Pour into an ice-cold tumbler and top with whipped cream or ice-cream. If preferred, flavour with a tablespoon of brandy or rum instead of vanilla.

1 egg
¼ pint (100 ml) milk
1 dessertspoon castor sugar
vanilla essence to taste
whipped cream or ice-cream

Advocaat Flip

Allow for each serving 2 tablespoons of advocaat, strained juice of one orange, and a little finely crushed ice. Blend at high speed and serve in custard goblets.

Banana Rum Egg-Nog

Beat egg yolks with sugar until the mixture is thick and light-coloured. In a blender, combine bananas, rum, and milk. Blend at high speed until smooth and pour the mixture over the egg yolks. Whisk to blend ingredients. Fold in cream and egg whites. Chill thoroughly and beat lightly before serving.

To make about 2 pints (1 litre) egg-nog:
3 raw egg yolks
2 tablespoons castor sugar
2 ripe, sliced bananas
4 oz (100 ml) light rum
6 oz (150 ml) milk
3 oz (75 ml) lightly whipped double cream
3 stiffly beaten egg whites

Coffee Flip, Barbados Style

Blend 2 eggs with 4 tablespoons vanilla flavoured (if liked) castor sugar until creamy and pale, gradually dilute with 1 pint (½ litre) cold milk. Add 6 oz (150 ml) coffee liqueur and a tablespoon of orange-blossom water. Blend well and decant into a chilled serving jug.

Egg Flip, Normandy Style
Pour 4 oz (100 ml) strained orange juice and an equal amount of Calvados into a blender, add a dessert-spoon castor sugar and 2 eggs. Blend well, decant into a chilled serving jug, add a spiral of orange peel, and serve.

Minty Lime or Lemon Drink

Good-size bunch of mint leaves
4 oz (100 g) sugar dissolved in ¼ pint (100 ml) boiling water
juice of 3 lemons
¼ pint (100 ml) lime or lemon juice
1 quart (1 litre) iced water
few drops of green colouring

Blend the mint leaves and hot, but not boiling, sugar syrup for a few minutes until the mint is well chopped. Strain. Mix fruit juices and colouring in the blender: add the mint-flavoured liquid. Pour into a large jug with iced water, stir well, and garnish with fresh mint.

Apricot Nectar

¼ lb (200 g) dried apricots, soaked overnight and then cooked in a sugar syrup until soft, or a tin of apricots, drained
juice of 1 lemon
water to dilute

Blend the drained apricots until smooth, gradually adding juice. Pour into a chilled jug, adding water if necessary for correct consistency.

Yoghurt Fruit Drinks
Put a carton of fruit-flavoured yoghourt and an equal quantity of cold milk into the goblet and run for a few seconds. For *Hazelnut and Ginger*: put a carton of hazel-nut-flavoured yoghurt into the blender with a little ginger ale. Run for a few seconds and serve at once.

Cosmetics
You can use your mixer or blender to make beauty preparations for yourself or to give away as presents. In the seventeenth and eighteenth centuries it was almost a tradition for cookery books to include recipes for beauty aids. Mrs Glasse in her 1747 edition of *The Art of Cookery Made Plain and Easy*, in addition to instructions on 'How to keep clear of Bugs' and 'A Certain Cure for the Bite of a Mad Dog', had a whole section of recipes for cosmetics. She gives admirable directions for making lip salve, almond pack for the face, and a skin lotion intriguingly named 'Virgin's Milk'.

There are some excellent old-fashioned and modern

recipes. By making them yourself you can control the purity of the ingredients, save money, and have fun.

An extra goblet would be useful to have, if you want to make scented cosmetics in your blender.

Deodorant
In a mixer combine one part of aluminium chloride crystals to three parts of water.

Cleansing Cream

4 oz (100 g) best lard
2 tablespoons rosewater
a few drops of perfume

Put lard in a bowl, cover with boiling water, leave until water becomes cold and lard floats up to the surface. Pour off water and repeat the process twice more.

Transfer lard to a clean basin, add rosewater, beat until creamy. Beat in a little perfume of your choice.

Cucumber and Honey Face Pack

½ cucumber
1 tablespoon clear honey
1 tablespoon almond oil
piece of butter muslin

Grate cucumber, combine with honey and almond oil, and mix well. Cut a piece of butter muslin large enough to cover the face, making two holes for eyes and one for mouth. Apply face pack, avoiding sensitive area round the eyes, cover with muslin mask, and leave for 15 minutes. Wipe off and sponge with warm water.

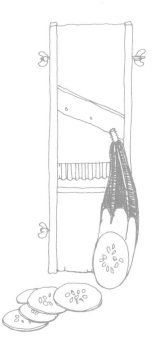

Anti-wrinkle Lotion
Blend 1 tablespoon glycerine, 1 tablespoon rosewater, 1½ tablespoons witch-hazel, and 3 tablespoons honey for 45 seconds.

Hand Lotion
Mix together in blender 1 tablespoon each almond oil and rosewater. Add yolk of an egg and run blender for further 45 seconds adding 50 drops tincture of benzoin, one drop at a time. (Use an eye dropper positioned in the hole of the drip feeder on top of the goblet.)

Papier-mâché Toys
And while we are being frivolous with the equipment, here is another idea suggested by the manufacturers. You can even use the blender to make papier-mâché

toys, if you have some talent as a sculptor, that is!

Tear newspapers into little pieces, cover with water, and soak overnight. To $\frac{1}{2}$ pint (250 ml) of wet paper add 1 pint ($\frac{1}{2}$ litre) of water and $\frac{1}{4}$ lb (100 g) of flour. Beat half the quantity at a time in the blender, then model into dolls or toys.

Clean the blender immediately after use.

SHREDDERS

We all know that many raw foods are good for us, but the trouble is that in their whole state some vegetables are not very exciting. Grated, shredded, or minced they are much more tempting, and electric shredders and mincers reduce the job to child's play.

Shredders can be obtained as an appliance, or as an attachment to a food mixer. They will shred most things. Usually a shredder is supplied with various-sized graters giving a choice of fine or coarse shredding. Sometimes a shredder has slicing blades as well, to enable the user to slice raw and cooked vegetables.

Appetizing salads are easily prepared. Vegetables like cucumbers are usually sliced thin, but carrots, celeriac, and other root vegetables should be shredded. A mixed salad looks good, especially if the ingredients are prepared in different ways – shredded, chopped, or grated. Cheese is excellent in salads and many kinds are suitable for shredding. Or you can mix several kinds of cheese, each cut up in a different way. Shredded raw mushrooms, leeks, carrots, peppers, onions, cabbage, radishes, cucumbers, celery, Brussels sprouts, chicory, celeriac, various cooked vegetables, coarsely grated nuts, pitted olives, and hard-boiled eggs are good for appetizing salads.

Recipes using Shredders

Carrot Soufflé

Combine egg yolks with onion, grated or minced carrots, orange flesh and rind. Gradually stir sauce into this mixture, check seasoning. Fold in egg whites, pour into a prepared soufflé dish, stand in a pan of hot water, and bake in the oven at 375 °F (190 °C) for 50 minutes. Serve in the same dish.

4 Servings
4 egg yolks
1 tablespoon grated onion
12 oz (300 g) raw grated carrot
shredded flesh of 1 orange
grated rind of 1 orange
¼ pint (250 ml) Béchamel sauce
*   (p. 143)*
salt
pepper
4 egg whites beaten stiff
butter for greasing dish

Coleslaw

Peel and shred apple, sprinkle immediately with lemon juice. Put carrot, walnuts, and sultanas through the shredder. Combine all ingredients in a salad bowl, season to taste, sprinkle with chopped parsley, dress with mayonnaise and serve.

4–6 Servings
1 small shredded cabbage
1 apple
1 tablespoon lemon juice
1 carrot
2 tablespoons peeled walnuts
2 tablespoons sultanas
1 teaspoon chopped parsley
seasoning
mayonnaise (p. 57)

Cheese and Walnut Salad

Shred cheese and walnuts as above, bind with mayonnaise, shape into balls, and arrange on crisp lettuce shells. Garnish with quartered hard-boiled eggs, sliced tomatoes, and cucumbers, and decorate with little sprigs of parsley.

Carrot Salad in Orange Shells

Peel the carrots, then grate or shred. Put in a bowl. Cut oranges in half, squeeze out all juice but do not break the orange shells.

Season carrots with salt and sugar, sprinkle in ginger and lemon juice, and pour on orange juice. Stir and chill for several hours.

Drain the carrot salad. (The marinating dressing can be strained and kept to be used again.)

Spoon the salad into orange shells, top with a slice of orange, and serve.

6 Servings
1 lb (½ kg) carrots
3 oranges
pinch salt
pinch sugar
1 tablespoon chopped fresh ginger
2 tablespoons lemon juice
6 peeled orange slices

Mincers and grinders can be obtained as separate appliances or as attachments to some food mixers. Mincers are designed to mince in the same way as a manual mincer and will mince cooked or raw meat and similar materials into small particles, usually by the action of a revolving 'feed scroll cup', cutting knives, and a perforated screen. Some models of mincers are provided with different-calibre mincing wheels. For lean raw meats small-hole wheels are recommended, which give a fine mince. The large-hole wheels are meant for cooked meats and for fat or sinewy cheaper cuts of raw meat.

Before using the mincer, grater or slicer cut the food into pieces which will fit into the machine. The easiest way to do this is with an electric carving knife, if you are fortunate in having one.

There are appliances which are slicers and graters combined. They have a special attachment with several interchangeable cones for fruits, vegetables, and cheese. The slicing cone is generally used for cabbage, carrots, potatoes, cucumbers, and cheese. The cone with large holes is good for white cabbage, julienne celery, carrots, and potatoes. The one with small holes is best for preparing cheeses such as cheddar for incorporating into sauces and for the fine shredding of vegetables for salads.

For harder foods you need a grinder. The attachment that comes with some models of mixers will pulverize coffee beans and all sorts of dry things, but if you want only the grinder, there are many kinds to choose from, with varying capacities.

COFFEE GRINDER AND MILL

Both the coffee grinder and the coffee mill can be purchased as a separate item or as an attachment to some food mixers. The coffee grinder is an appliance in which coffee beans are supplied from a container to a grinding system consisting of two grinding discs or cones, one rotating and one fixed. After the coffee has been ground it leaves the grinding system. Very often the size of coffee may be varied by a mechanical adjustment, or by altering the clearance between the top discs. Don't overfill the bowl. It is better to grind in two or three batches. The results are better and you don't run the risk of overloading the mechanism.

The coffee mill is usually an appliance in which the coffee beans are broken by means of cutting blades at high speeds in a container. Normally the contents remain in this container and the size of the ground coffee is reduced by increasing the operating time.

The degree of fineness you get depends on how long the machine is operated. You soon learn to hold down the lid all the time the motor is on, otherwise the ingredients can fly about. Never run the grinder when it is empty, and never run the grinder longer than the period specified by the manufacturers. After use, unplug and simply wipe the bowl with soft kitchen paper or a dry cloth.

Very often a coffee mill will also make breadcrumbs, grind spices, and make castor sugar from granulated sugar. It will even grate cheese.

Recipes using Mincers and Grinders

Chopped Liver, Israeli Style

Fry onion in fat until transparent. Slice and fry livers until very brown on both sides. Mince livers, onion, egg whites (reserving yolks) twice. Add sugar and seasoning to taste. Moisten with a little melted chicken fat. Spread evenly on a flat plate. Mash egg yolks and sprinkle over liver.

To freeze, after seasoning spoon chopped liver into a rigid container, pour a little chicken fat on top, leave a head space, seal, and freeze.

Before using, thaw out in refrigerator, put in a serving dish, sprinkle with chopped hard-boiled egg, and serve with hot toast.

6 Servings
1 lb (½ kg) chicken livers (or ox livers or a combination of both)
1 large, sliced Spanish onion
2 hard-boiled eggs
¼ teaspoon sugar
salt and pepper
chicken fat or oil

Smoked Haddock Soufflé

Steam the haddock in a little milk between two plates over boiling water. As soon as it is done, strain and keep the liquid. Discard any bones or skin.

Put the fish through a mincer (or purée in a blender). Pre-heat oven to 350 °F (180 °C). Heat 1 oz (25 g) butter, stir in flour, cook for a few minutes to amalgamate, without browning. Dilute gradually with warmed milk, add liquid in which the haddock was steamed, lemon rind, and seasoning. Simmer, stirring until the sauce thickens.

Remove from heat, add fish and stir in yolks. Whisk the whites into a stiff foam, fold into haddock mixture, and pour into lightly buttered 8–9 in. (20–23 cm) soufflé dish. Dot with tiny pieces of butter and bake for 18–20 minutes. Serve with anchovy sauce.

To make anchovy sauce, put Béchamel sauce through a blender with 5–6 anchovy fillets until smooth.

4 Servings
8 oz (200 g) smoked haddock
2 oz (50 g) butter
1 oz (25 g) flour
½ pint (250 ml) milk
¼ teaspoon grated lemon rind
salt and pepper
3 raw yolks
3 egg whites

Hamburgers

Hamburgers are great favourites with the young and – served with mashed potatoes, grilled tomatoes or mushrooms, and a crisp salad – can make an excellent snack or supper meal.

Put the beef and onion through the mincer. Season to taste, add herbs and egg, and mix well.

Shape into flat cakes and fry in a little fat until brown on both sides. Do not overcook.

6 Servings
1½ lb (750 g) beef
1 large onion
salt and pepper
pinch mixed herbs
1–2 eggs, depending on size
fat for frying, shallow

Steak Tartare

4 Servings
1 lb (½ kg) lean, raw rump steak
salt and black pepper
4 egg yolks
capers, gherkins, chopped shallots, and
  parsley to garnish

Using the fine cutter, put meat through mincer, then mix with salt, freshly ground black pepper, and egg yolks. Form into four flat round cakes and serve garnished with capers, gherkins, chopped shallots, and parsley.

Waldorf Salad

4 Servings
2 large eating apples
2 teaspoons lemon juice
2 oz (50 g) walnuts
4 tablespoons chopped celery
4 tablespoons mayonnaise
lettuce leaves

Core apples and cut into small cubes. Sprinkle with lemon juice. Chop celery and nuts in chopper. Mix all the ingredients with mayonnaise, sweeten to taste, and serve on a bed of lettuce leaves.

Moussaka

3 Servings for 4 people
3 lb (1½ kg) minced beef, lamb or
  veal
5–6 medium-sized aubergines
sea salt and pepper
olive oil
2 oz (50 g) dripping
1 finely chopped onion
4 oz (100 g) ripe, peeled sliced
  tomatoes
1 tablespoon chopped parsley
1 gill (100 ml) red wine
2 tablespoons butter
3 oz (75 g) grated cheese
1 pint (½ litre) cheese sauce (p. 143)
½ teaspoon grated nutmeg

Mince the meat. Remove stalks from aubergines, slice, and sprinkle them generously with sea salt. Leave to stand for an hour, to draw away bitterness. Rinse, drain, dry on a cloth, and fry in oil till brown on both sides. Remove, drain, and keep warm.

Heat half the dripping and fry the onion until it becomes soft, add meat, and brown quickly. Add tomatoes, parsley, seasoning to taste, moisten with wine, and simmer gently for 10 minutes. Remove from heat, add 2 to 3 tablespoons sauce and mix well. Grease an oven-proof dish, line it with one-third of the aubergine slices, purple side downwards. Proceed to fill the dish with alternate layers of mince and slices of fried aubergine, sprinkling each layer with cheese and a few tiny pieces of butter, until you use up one-third of these ingredients. Press well down in the dish. Cover with aubergine skins, purple side up. Flavour sauce with nutmeg, pour it over the dish, sprinkle the top with grated cheese, dot with small pieces of butter, and bake in a moderately hot oven 400 °F (200 °C) for 40–45 minutes.

Let the dish stand for a few minutes, then turn out on to a serving dish and serve. Or serve the moussaka in the same dish, as it comes out of the oven.

To freeze, divide remaining two-thirds of all ingredients between two foil dishes, packing them in as you did for baking, the one-third portion to be served immediately. Sprinkle the tops with grated cheese, seal in double thickness of foil wrap, and freeze.

To serve, uncover and bake as above.

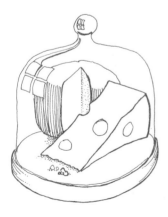

Italian Minced Veal in Almond Sauce

4 Servings
½ lb (200 g) cooked veal or lamb
salt and pepper
1 egg
2 oz (50 g) ground almonds
1 tablespoon chopped parsley
½ pint (250 ml) water
2 tablespoons olive oil
juice of ½ lemon

Mince the meat, put into mixing bowl, season well, bind with egg, blend thoroughly, and shape into small balls. Put almonds in a pan, add parsley and water, bring to the boil, season, incorporate oil and, as soon as boiling is re-established, drop in the meat balls. Make sure they are covered with the liquid, reduce heat, and simmer under a lid for 1 hour. Taste for seasoning, heighten with a dash of lemon juice, and serve very hot with rice or mashed potatoes.

To freeze, stand the pan in a bowl of iced water to cool quickly. Put into rigid container, leaving a head space, seal, and freeze. Reheat unthawed in an oven-proof dish at 400 °F (200 °C) for about 1 hour, until throughly heated. Check seasoning before serving.

ROTISSERIE

Kebab cookery is by the quick, high-temperature method. But, as with the big spit, it is quite satisfactory to reduce the heat and leave skewered meat rotating gently until the other food is ready – something which is not really advisable with conventional grills. Sausages, liver, and kidneys can all be cooked on it, but steak used for kebabs goes further with the addition of mushrooms, bacon, onion, and tomatoes. For rugged appetites, unload the whole kebab into a hunk of hot French bread.

Not only meat, fish, and poultry, but many vegetables and fruits can be cooked on the rotisserie. The kebab attachment is excellent for tomatoes, onions, mushrooms, sweet corn, and courgettes. Bananas and mandarins can also be threaded on skewers.

GRILLING TIMES

Bacon rashers	3–5 minutes
Steak, 1½ in. (4 cm) thick, medium rare	12–15 minutes
Gammon, according to thickness	10–15 minutes
Kidneys	5–10 minutes
Liver, according to thickness	5–10 minutes
Mushrooms	5–10 minutes
Sausages	10–12 minutes
Tomatoes, halved	8–10 minutes
Lamb chops, according to thickness	10–15 minutes
Pork or veal chops	15–20 minutes

ROASTING TIMES

Poultry and white meat, up to 3 lb (1½ kg)
25 minutes per lb (or ½ kg)
Poultry and white meat over 3 lb (1½ kg)
20 minutes per lb (or ½ kg)
Pork, up to 3 lb (1½ kg)   30 minutes per lb (or ½ kg)
Pork, over 3 lb (1½ kg)   25 minutes per lb (or ½ kg)
Red meat, up to 2 lb (1 kg)
15 minutes per lb (or ½ kg)
Red meat, 2 to 4 lb (1–2 kg)
12 minutes per lb (or ½ kg)
Red meat, over 4 lb (2 kg)
10 minutes per lb (or ½ kg)

The times given are approximate and will vary according to the roast, its quality, and your personal taste. As a rule allow 5 minutes' pre-heating at full heat. Cooking is normally at full heat. If required, switch to low.

Recipes using Rotisserie and Kebab Attachment

Mixed Grill

Trim the cutlets, removing surplus fat. Skin the kidneys, cut almost in half without actually separating them, cut out membranes, wash, and dry. Prick sausages with a fork. Cut off bacon rinds. Remove mushroom stalks and wipe the mushrooms with a soft cloth. Season all ingredients to taste, brush with melted butter. Grease the grid of the grill and see that the grill is really hot. Grill the cutlets, kidneys, and the sausages first for about 5 minutes, add bacon, tomatoes, and mushrooms, and cook until done, brushing the meats with melted butter from time to time and turning. Arrange on a heated dish, put a piece of maître d'hôtel butter on each portion of meat, garnish with watercress and lemon wedges, and serve.

4 Servings
4 lamb cutlets
4 lamb's kidneys
4 chipolata sausages
4 halved tomatoes
4 rashers bacon
8 mushrooms
salt and pepper
melted butter
4 oz (100 g) maître d'hôtel butter
(p. 60)
watercress for garnish
1 lemon cut in wedges

Barbecued Christmas Ham with Rum Sauce

Put the ham on a spit, attach to cooking mechanism, and roast over medium heat, allowing 10 minutes per pound (or ½ kg).

Blend all the other ingredients, heat, and use for basting ham. When done, place the ham on a heated serving dish. Combine drip-pan juices with any remaining basting liquid, heat, and serve as sauce.

Serve lettuce and pineapple salad separately.

5 lb (2¼ kg) shoulder ham
4 tablespoons rum
4 tablespoons pineapple juice
1 tablespoon lemon juice
1 teaspoon dry mustard
1 teaspoon treacle or golden syrup
1 teaspoon powdered ginger
1 crushed clove ginger
pinch pepper

Roast Chicken

The best way of roasting any poultry is on the spit. Adjust the heat as indicated and the bird will be browned on the outside and cooked on the inside at the same time.

See timetable at the beginning of this chapter for roasting chicken.

Spit-roasted poultry should be basted frequently with the fat which collects in a layer just above the gravy in the dripping pan.

Note: Make sure frozen poultry and joints are completely thawed before cooking.

Brochettes

There is a vast number of these dishes cooked on skewers and they include many classical French specialities, the Russian shashlyk, the kebabs of Near, Middle, and Far East, etc. Many kinds of meat, fish and vegetables are suitable and this is where the kebab attachment is invaluable, because by its regular turning it ensures uniform cooking and self-basting. It is a good way to make a small amount of meat go a long way, as you can intersperse pieces of meat with slices of bacon, onion, tomato, mushroom, etc. Don't string the ingredients too tightly, because this will prevent heat from penetrating between them.

It is usual to marinate the meats before cooking and the marinades can vary.

Here is a basic recipe, which you can vary according to ingredients available.

Lamb Kebab

6 Servings
2 lb (1 kg) lamb (best end of neck)
1 large finely sliced onion
1–2 tablespoons chopped parsley
salt and pepper
1 tablespoon sherry (optional)
1–2 tablespoons oil
juice of ½ lemon
a little butter

Trim all fat off meat and cut it into 1 in. (2 cm) cubes. Put in a bowl, sprinkle with the rest of the ingredients, and leave to marinate for an hour, turning from time to time. Thread on greased skewers, leaving ½ in (1 cm) space between each piece of meat. Brush with a little melted butter (or oil) and grill for 5–6 minutes.

Serve with rice and salad.

Grilled Kidneys

Follow the above recipe, using halved lamb or sheep kidneys, thread on skewers with pieces of onion, streaky bacon, small whole mushrooms, and tomatoes.

Liver Kebab

As above using pieces of lamb or calf liver. Or use halved pieces of chicken liver wrapped in a rasher of streaky bacon.

Mixed Kebab

Use any combination of any of the ingredients of the above three recipes.

Grilled Poussin

Each of the poussins (young chickens) serves two

people. If you use a frozen poussin, defrost to room temperature before grilling.

Cut the poussin down the back, if not already cut through. Flatten it out and slip the wing tips around the wings, as you would for roasting. Run two long skewers through the legs and body and wings to hold the flattened poussin in position.

Place in the grill pan, skin side up, and brush with melted butter. Grill gently – at a medium heat – for the bird will burn easily. Give it up to 10 minutes, depending on its thickness, basting twice in that time. Turn, brush generously with more butter, and grill again.

Meanwhile, add a teaspoon of Worcester sauce to a little French mustard mixed with a little water. Pour into the grill pan and heat through. Remove the skewers from the poussin and cut through the breast with kitchen scissors to divide the bird in two. Place on a hot platter, pour the sauce over it, and serve garnished with watercress and game chips.

DEEP FAT FRIERS

Scotch Eggs

4 Servings
1 lb (½ kg) sausage meat
4 hard-boiled eggs
seasoned flour
egg and breadcrumbs
fat for frying

Divide sausage meat into four portions. Shell eggs, dip into seasoned flour, and coat each egg with a portion of the sausage meat. Coat each sausage-covered egg with beaten egg and then with the breadcrumbs.

Fry (fairly slowly so that the sausage meat is cooked through) for 8–10 minutes, until golden-brown.

When cold, cut in half and serve with a salad.

Whitebait

6 Servings
2¼–3 lb (1–1¼ kg) whitebait
flour
deep fat for frying
salt
cayenne pepper
lemon

Keep the whitebait on ice until ready to cook.

Heat fat to correct temperature.

Dry the whitebait on a cloth, dredge lightly with flour.

Put a small portion of whitebait in a wire basket, shake off surplus flour, and plunge into hot fat for 3–4 minutes, shaking the basket frequently.

Lift the basket, shake to drain off fat, turn whitebait on to absorbent kitchen paper, and keep warm. Continue to fry the rest of the fish. Season with fine dry salt and cayenne pepper and serve with lemon cut into wedges.

Fish Croquettes

4–5 Servings
1 lb (½ kg) white fish
2–3 slices of crustless bread
2–3 tablespoons milk
1 small onion
salt and pepper
2 eggs
1–2 tablespoons flour
breadcrumbs
oil for deep frying

Skin the fish and remove bones, if any.

Soak the bread in a little milk.

Put the fish, onion, and bread through a mincer. Season to taste, add one egg, and mix well.

Shape into croquettes, dip in flour, then in beaten egg and breadcrumbs.

Deep fry in hot fat until crisp and brown. Avoid too high a heat, otherwise you will find the croquettes too dark on the outside without being cooked properly on the inside. Drain on kitchen paper. Serve with anchovy sauce.

Leek and Beef Croquettes

4 Servings
1 lb (½ kg) cooked leeks
4 oz (100 g) cooked beef
1 chopped hard-boiled egg
salt and pepper
1 beaten egg
breadcrumbs

Put leeks, beef, and hard-boiled egg together through a mincer. Season to taste, mix well, and bind with beaten egg. Taking a little of the mixture at a time, shape into balls the size of a walnut. Lightly roll in breadcrumbs. Heat oil, deep fry the croquettes, drain on kitchen paper, and serve.

To freeze, after rolling in breadcrumbs, pack uncooked croquettes in a double thickness of foil, or in a suitable rigid container with a well-fitting lid. Put a sheet of cellophane paper between each layer. Seal and freeze. To use, take out the required number of frozen croquettes and, without thawing, deep fry and serve as described.

Chicken à la Kiev

Remove the four fillets, taking off breast and wing for each portion. (The rest of the chickens can be used for another dish.) Skin and carefully bone the fillets in such a way as to keep each in one piece and to leave a small bone attached to each fillet.

Beat fillets to flatten and season.

Cut butter into uniform 'fingers', season, roll slightly to give them cigar shapes, and chill thoroughly.

Put a piece of frozen seasoned butter on each fillet, fold the flesh over it, and roll up the fillet neatly into a cigar shape with the bone sticking out at one end. It is essential to enclose the butter completely. Dip in beaten egg, roll in breadcrumbs. Do this twice to make the coating adhere and to seal the butter inside it.

Heat the oil and deep fry the chicken for 4–5 minutes, until uniformly golden. Before serving put a paper frill on each bone. Garnish with lemon wedges and watercress. This is eminently suitable for freezing and provides a reserve of a splendid dish for special occasions.

To freeze, after coating with egg and breadcrumbs, pack in a suitable plastic box, put cellophane paper between layers, cover closely, seal, and freeze.

Before using, thaw overnight in refrigerator. Then deep fry and serve as described.

Jam Doughnuts

Mix yeast with milk and stir to dissolve. Blend castor sugar and butter until light and creamy. Whisk in eggs. Add salt, vanilla, and nutmeg and beat well. Add flour and little by little work in milk with yeast. Knead until the dough is smooth. Cover with a cloth and leave in a warm place to rise, which should take from 2 to $2\frac{1}{2}$ hours.

Turn out on to a lightly floured board, knead lightly for 5–6 minutes. Divide dough into 24 pieces, roll each into a small ball, flatten, and put $\frac{1}{2}$ teaspoon of jam in

oil for deep frying

4 Servings
2 small frying chickens
6 oz (150 g) butter
salt and pepper
2 beaten eggs
breadcrumbs
oil for deep frying

To make 2 dozen doughnuts:
2 oz (50 g or 2 cakes) yeast
$\frac{1}{2}$ pint (250 ml) lukewarm milk
4 oz (100 g) castor sugar
2 oz (50 g) butter or margarine
2 eggs
1 teaspoon salt
1 teaspoon vanilla
$\frac{1}{4}$ teaspoon nutmeg
1 lb ($\frac{1}{2}$ kg) flour
jam
oil for deep frying
icing sugar

the middle. Enclose the jam and reshape the dough into a ball again. Leave on a floured board for 15–20 minutes. Heat oil and deep fry doughnuts a few at a time, turning them once until golden-brown all over. Drain on kitchen paper.

Mix icing sugar with cinnamon, and dust the doughnuts with the mixture.

To freeze, cook as described, cool, leave uncovered, chill. Pack into a suitable plastic or foil box, with a piece of cellophane paper between layers. Seal and freeze.

To serve, heat through in the oven pre-heated to 400 °F (200 °C).

4 oz (100 g) flour
pinch of salt
1 egg
¼ pint (100 ml) milk
apples

Apple Fritters

Sieve the flour and salt, break the egg into the flour. Whisk and gradually add the milk until a smooth batter is formed. Peel and core apples and slice into rings. Dip into batter, deep fry for 3–5 minutes at about 350 °F (180 °C) until golden-brown.

Banana Fritters

As above, using sliced bananas instead of apples.

REFRIGERATORS

Refrigerators are designed to keep perishable foods safe from harmful changes in temperature and humidity. Left-over foods can be kept for several days with complete safety, at the right temperature.

There are two types of refrigerator. The most common is the compressor type. In this, the vapour is compressed and changes back into liquid when passed through a condenser. The electric motor and compressor are usually hermetically sealed in one unit and need no attention. Because of speedier reduction in temperature and ability to obtain lower temperatures this is the system most generally used today.

Smaller domestic refrigerators are sometimes of the absorption type. This type has no moving parts and is operated by the external application of a small amount of heat.

Almost all refrigerators have a knob which varies the thermostat setting to maintain the correct temperature in the frozen-food storage compartment. A one-star marking means that at normal setting frozen food can be stored for up to one week (maximum temperature -6 °C); a two-star marking means that frozen food can be stored for up to one month (maximum temperature -12 °C); and a three-star marking means that frozen food can be stored for up to three months (maximum temperature -18 °C).

On some cabinets you will need to keep the control knob set to maximum to achieve the right temperature, but on most it is usually somewhere halfway and only needs turning up in hot weather, or if installed in a warm area such as a centrally heated kitchen.

The best plan for most families is to pick a good, modest-sized refrigerator, and plan space for a food freezer rather than try to get along with a fridge with a 1 or 2 cubic feet three-star compartment that is capable of freezing.

Choose the refrigerator by using the old rule of 1 cu ft for each member of the family and 1 extra. Double this formula for the food freezer and treat the total cubic capacity as the minimum for your needs. Where space is very limited, one of the tall, front-opening freezers that take up the minimum of floor area of a combined refrigerator and food freezer may be a solution.

Many of the new refrigerators have simple defrosting methods. The refrigerator has to work harder to maintain satisfactory temperatures if layers of ice form. So most cabinets need defrosting at least once a fortnight, and some models once a week.

Never let the layer of ice on the outside of the evaporator become thicker than $\frac{1}{4}$ in. ($\frac{1}{2}$ cm). If you do, you reduce the efficiency of the refrigeration and waste electricity.

Many refrigerators have push-button defrosting. With this system you should empty the frozen-food storage section, because in some models pressing the button directs heat into the cabinet so that the ice melts quickly. As the cabinet switches itself on again automatically, all you need to do is empty the drip tray. As the defrosting process is rapid, frozen food will not come to any harm if it is kept well wrapped in newspapers and returned as soon as defrosting is completed.

Automatic defrosting melts accumulated ice at regular intervals and channels the water into a drip tray, from which it evaporates.

There are a few simple rules for looking after and getting the most out of your refrigerator.

Never try to hasten the defrosting by chipping off the ice or 'snow'. This may damage the mechanism. Follow manufacturer's instructions for cleaning your refrigerator and, should any problem arise, call a specialist.

To avoid condensation never put hot or warm food into a refrigerator.

Wrap food, especially products with a strong smell such as fish, in plastic wrap or foil.

Many models have separate compartments for milk, cheese, butter, and eggs. Use them as indicated for maximum efficiency. Always keep milk and cream covered whether in bottles or jugs.

Raw meat is best kept lightly covered to allow circulation of air round it; cooked meat in foil or plastic. Both plastic bags and boxes are good and stop the meat getting dry.

Certain fruit – melons, pineapples, and bananas – are not suitable for storage in a refrigerator. They cause all the other food to become tainted with a disagreeable smell. You can, however, put them in for a short time to chill just before serving. Always put salads and vegetables in plastic boxes, or keep in the drawer intended for salads.

Use your refrigerator space rationally. There is no point in cluttering it up with plates and dishes. Economize on the size of your containers. Whenever possible simply wrap food with foil or keep in a polythene bag.

To keep your food fresh and wholesome, make sure you leave enough space for the air to circulate. Don't stuff the refrigerator chock-a-block.

FROZEN-FOOD COMPARTMENT

The popularity and variety of frozen food makes an ever greater demand on frozen-food storage. I have already dealt with the star marking system which indicates how long frozen food can be stored in a given refrigerator. Remember that the frozen-food storage compartment is not designed to do the job of a home freezer, which I deal with in detail in the next chapter.

You cannot expect to keep frozen food in a frozen-food compartment indefinitely. Watch the instructions on the packets to make sure you don't keep any product longer than recommended.

Frozen food which has been allowed to thaw completely should be used as fresh food. Do not refreeze it unless ice crystals are still present.

Don't keep empty ice-cube trays in the refrigerator. As you use up the cubes, fill the trays with water and replace.

We have now finished with the strictly practical side of the refrigerator. It is, of course, a great advantage to know that with its help you can store your food in complete safety – provided you follow the common-sense rules. But the refrigerator can bring glamour to the kitchen. You can use it for making many attractive dishes, which would be impossible otherwise, from chilled soups and aspics to cold soufflés and ice-cream. Recipes for all these and many others are given in this section, and for a further selection of recipes for which a refrigerator is essential, *see* the Blender and Freezer Sections.

Dishes for the Refrigerator

Jellied Tarragon Eggs
Arrange soft-boiled or poached eggs in moulds coated with tarragon-flavoured aspic jelly. Fill the moulds with jelly and chill to set.

Turn the eggs out at the last moment, arrange in a circle, fill the centre with chopped jelly.

Avocado Gazpacho
This cold avocado soup, with mixed vegetables, makes a delicious and refreshing summer starting course. Particularly good served with hot garlic bread.

For garnish

Pass the avocado and onions through a blender with wine, lemon juice, and water. Add sugar, season to taste with salt and pepper, transfer to a bowl and chill.

Make sure tomatoes, peppers, and cucumber are cut in uniform small dice. Mix this garnish and chill.

Serve the gazpacho iced, in individual bowls, topped with a portion of mixed, diced vegetables.

6 Servings
1 lb (½ kg) avocado flesh
2 sliced, medium-sized onions
8 oz (200 ml) dry white wine
juice of 1 lemon
8 oz (200 ml) iced water
1 teaspoon sugar
1 teaspoon salt
black pepper

2 oz (50 g) peeled, diced tomatoes
2 oz (50 g) seeded, diced green peppers
2 oz (50 g) diced cucumber

Veal in Aspic
This is an excellent way of presenting veal for a cold buffet.

Pour a thin layer of aspic jelly into a mould, tilt it to line bottom and sides, and put in a refrigerator. As soon as the jelly lining the mould sets, decorate bottom and sides with slices of hard-boiled egg, olives, and cucumber. Spoon a little jelly to secure these decorations and chill until they set.

Put veal in the middle of the mould, season, garnish with carrots and peas, sprinkle with parsley, spoon over some aspic jelly to seal down these ingredients, and chill to set them. Add the rest of the aspic jelly. Chill until set hard, preferably overnight.

To serve, dip mould for a moment into warm water, wipe, and turn out on to a chilled dish.

If you have any aspic left over, pour it into a shallow mould and leave until firm, then cut the jelly into triangles or 'wolf's teeth' croûtons.

Serve with lemon wedges and freshly grated horseradish.

To freeze, after the aspic is set hard, cover with foil, seal, and freeze.

To serve, thaw overnight in refrigerator.

2 Servings for 4 people
aspic jelly (p. 108)
3 hard-boiled eggs
3 tablespoons sliced stuffed olives
1–2 sliced pickled cucumbers
3 lb (1½ kg) cold roast fillet of veal
salt and pepper
3 tablespoons diced cooked carrots
3 tablespoons cooked peas
1 tablespoon chopped parsley
lemon wedges
horseradish

Chicken in Aspic

4–6 Servings
3 pints (1¾ litres) liquid aspic jelly
(see below)
3 lb (1½ kg) chicken
tarragon leaves

Prepare stock for aspic jelly as described and poach the chicken in it until tender. Make sure there is enough stock to immerse the chicken completely.

Remove the chicken and leave to cool.

Strain the aspic and leave until it begins to look syrupy, without allowing it to set.

Divide the chicken into portions, skin them, and lay out on a grid placed over a dish. Space the pieces so they do not touch. Coat each portion with several layers of aspic, spooning it over them and letting each layer set before applying the next. Transfer chicken portions to a serving dish, decorate with tarragon leaves, spoon over them the remaining aspic jelly and any that has collected in the dish, and chill in refrigerator.

Chicken Salad in Cranberry Ring

6–8 Servings
1 tablespoon unflavoured gelatine
3 tablespoons cold water
1 lb (500 ml) cranberry sauce
3 tablespoons lemon juice
¼ teaspoon grated lemon rind
8 oz (200 g) cooked, diced chicken
4 oz (100 g) diced celery
4 oz (100 g) pineapple cubes
salad dressing
lettuce

Dissolve gelatine in cold water. Crush the cranberry sauce with a fork, add lemon juice and rind and the dissolved gelatine. Blend, pour into a ring mould, and chill until set. Combine the chicken, celery, and pineapple, add dressing, mix carefully, leave it to stand for 30 minutes and chill.

Unmould the cranberry border on to a lettuce-lined dish. Spoon the chicken salad into the middle and serve.

Quick Aspic Jelly

1 pint (½ litre) stock (p. 139)
1 teaspoon chopped tarragon
2–3 sprigs parsley
juice of 1 lemon
10 peppercorns
1 chopped shallot (or ½ onion)
½ bay leaf
1 oz (25 g) gelatine
3 tablespoons sherry (or Madeira)
salt
1 egg white and shell

Boil the stock with tarragon, parsley, lemon juice, peppercorns, shallot, and bay leaf for 10 minutes. Dissolve the gelatine in 2 tablespoons of cold water and add to the stock. Simmer for 5 minutes, add sherry and salt to taste, and strain. To clarify the jelly bring the stock to the boil. Beat the egg white and crush the shell and add both to the stock. Simmer for 5 minutes, strain once again, and use or freeze as described in recipes for stock.

Cucumber and Cream Cheese Mousse

4 Servings
cucumbers
1 tablespoon gelatine
1 tablespoon chopped chives
12 oz (300 g) cream cheese
salt and white pepper
lettuce

Peel, seed, and grate enough cucumbers to make ½ pint (250 ml) pulp. Drain off the juice and soften gelatine in it for 5 minutes, then dissolve completely over hot water, cool, and add to cucumber. Add chives, stir and chill the mixture until it starts to thicken.

Beat the cheese until smooth and add to cucumber mixture. Blend well, season to taste, pour into a mould rinsed in cold water and chill. Unmould the mousse on to a chilled dish and serve on lettuce leaves garnished with cucumber slices.

For freezing, instead of pouring into a mould, spoon into a rigid container or individual prepared cases, leaving a small head space, seal, and freeze.

For serving, thaw at room temperature, unmould, garnish, and serve as described.

Refrigerator Cheesecake (No Cooking)

Mix biscuit crumbs with butter, 1 tablespoon sugar and cinnamon, and use mixture to line a hinged flan tin.

Drain pineapple and keep the juice. In a double boiler, mix 4 oz (100 g) sugar, salt, 1 gill (100 ml) pineapple juice, egg yolks, and cook over boiling water until smooth and thickened, stirring constantly.

Soak gelatine in cold water for 5 minutes, add to mixture in double boiler, and stir until dissolved, then chill the mixture until it begins to set. Add pineapple, cheese, and lemon rind and juice. Fold in egg whites and whipped cream. Pour into flan tin, smooth the top, chill for 10–12 hours and serve.

To freeze, cover chilled cheesecake with double foil wrap and freeze. Before serving, thaw at room temperature or in a refrigerator, without unwrapping.

2 oz (50 g) wholewheat biscuit crumbs
2 tablespoons melted butter
sugar
¼ teaspoon cinnamon
1 small fresh (or tinned crushed) pineapple
pinch salt
3 lightly beaten egg yolks
2 tablespoons gelatine
4 tablespoons cold water
1 lb (½ kg) cream cheese
1 teaspoon lemon rind
2 tablespoons lemon juice
3 stiffly beaten egg whites
¼ pint (250 ml) whipped cream

Ice-cream Custard

Put cream and flavouring into a double boiler, stir in egg yolks, heat, stirring all the time over simmering water until the mixture thickens. Remove from heat, but continue to stir for a few minutes. Add sugar, stir to dissolve and blend in, allow to cool, strain, and use as required.

6 Servings
12 oz (300 ml) very fresh cream
flavouring (vanilla bean, thinly cut lemon or orange peel, etc.)
4 egg yolks
4 oz (100 g) icing sugar (or pounded castor sugar)

Vanilla Ice-cream

Beat the egg yolks and dilute with a little milk. Scald the rest of the milk with vanilla, salt, and sugar and heat to dissolve, stirring all the time. Remove from heat, one by one stir in egg yolks, pour mixture into a double saucepan, cook until the mixture thickens over simmering water (8–10 minutes), stirring constantly. When the mixture coats the back of a wooden spoon, remove from heat (i.e. take the pan with the custard

6 egg yolks
1¼ pints (¾ litre) milk
1 teaspoon vanilla
pinch salt
10 oz (250 g) sugar
¼ pint (250 ml) whipped cream

mixture out of hot water), stir to cool. Strain, add whipped cream, and freeze.

To prepare ice-cream for the freezer, after adding whipped cream, put in rigid containers, leaving a small head space, seal, and freeze.

Before use, thaw in refrigerator until soft and serve with chocolate sauce.

Almond Ice-cream
Make vanilla ice-cream mixture (*as above*), add 4 oz (100 g) almonds and 4 bitter almonds, blanched and pounded with 2–3 tablespoons water. Mix well and freeze.

Strawberry Ice-cream
Prepare ice-cream mixture as described, add the sieved pulp from 1 lb ($\frac{1}{2}$ kg) of fresh strawberries, and proceed as described.

(Redcurrants and other soft fruit can also be used for ice-cream.)

Coffee Ice-cream
Add 4 oz (100 g) freshly roasted coffee beans to the uncooked custard mixture. Cook as desired. When the custard thickens to the desired consistency, remove from heat and leave to infuse for 2–3 hours. Strain and freeze as described.

Chocolate Ice-cream
Dissolve 6 oz (150 g) grated chocolate in the milk intended for ice-cream custard (*see vanilla ice-cream*). Make the custard as usual and freeze.

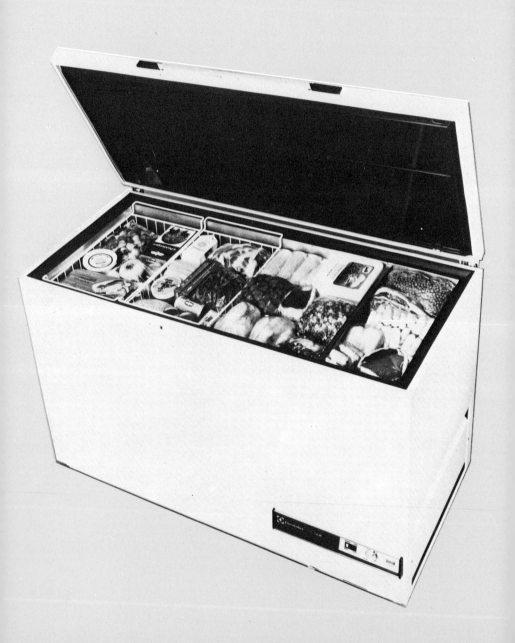

Why bother to freeze food?

People have been concerned with preserving food since time immemorial. One of the oldest European cookery books, written 2,000 years ago by Apicius, devotes some thought to the subject. Apicius, who was the greatest cookery expert of Ancient Rome – he lived under Augustus and Tiberius – gives practical advice on keeping meat fresh. His recipe is to cover meat with honey and hang it in a draught. He says: 'This is better in winter; in the summer it will keep only a few days.'

Nothing silly about that advice. The honey would seal in the meat the way polythene does; the moisture in it would provide a certain amount of evaporation, and being suspended in the breeze, if any, would help.

The reason for this age-old concern is obvious. One would be safe eating freshly caught fish, but if kept it can quickly become lethal, because of its rapid deterioration. The moment an animal is killed, or fruit or a vegetable picked, it is dead and loses its resistance to becoming spoiled. Anyone who has thrown away a stale vegetable must have noticed its musty smell and loss of colour and texture.

The Eskimos, Siberians, and other Arctic dwellers have long practised freezing as a method of preserving fish and game for long periods of time.

Freezing is the best, quickest, and safest method of preserving food because it inhibits the growth of micro-organisms which cause decay. Food frozen at the correct temperature is more like fresh food in texture, flavour, and colour than food preserved by any other way.

Freezing has a further advantage over other methods of food preservation, from the housewife's point of view, in that it is the easiest method which can be used in the home.

Only freezing at the correct low temperature will give the results you need. The temperature of 32 °F (0 °C) at which ice melts, is insufficient. It will keep food wholesome for a brief period, but natural spoilage is certain to follow. For safe, satisfactory freezing you need temperatures not higher than 0 °F (-18 °C). Industrial freezing of food is done at even lower temperatures (*see Frozen Food Temperature Chart*).

In the correct rapid-freezing process the crystals form actually within the cells of the freezing food. If it is frozen slowly, liquid oozes from them and is mixed with the ice forming between the cells. Slow freezing

affects adversely the texture of food, and a sure sign is the amount of liquid running out when the food is thawed.

With this lost fluid, you lose the eating qualities of the food, particularly of vegetables. For the same reasons, manufacturers of frozen foods advise putting vegetables unthawed into boiling water. They need rapid thawing, so do not take out a packet of frozen vegetables and leave it lying around, unless you are ready to cook it at once. Other foods need to be thawed out slowly at room temperature. Instructions for thawing are given in individual recipes of various dishes and should be strictly followed.

The advantages of a food freezer

Freezing saves time and money. You can do your shopping once a week, or once a month, instead of every day.

You can prepare any dish in sufficient quantities for several meals; serve one and freeze the rest for future use. Reheating say, a casserole, takes less time than cooking it from scratch.

If you live in the country and are lucky enough to have produce of your own, you can freeze it during seasons of plenty. If you live in the town, take advantage of the times when there is a glut of the more expensive fruit and vegetables, buy and freeze them when the prices are lower.

You can save more money by bulk buying. This is particularly so in the case of fresh meat. Suppliers of frozen foods will deliver them to you in refrigerated vans at reduced prices, sometimes at nearly half-price, if you buy in bulk.

There are also 'cash and carry' frozen-food depots where you can buy one or two items at bulk prices or collect a small order once every month or so. Take advantage, too, of 'special offers' of frozen food in your supermarket; 'pick them yourself' farm offers during country weekends; and end-of-day bargains in the markets. In these ways the freezer will help you to cater and budget more economically.

You can stock up your freezer with cooked dishes, which you can prepare whenever it suits you. With a variety of ready-made soups, casseroles, pastry, sauces, desserts, and cakes, catering for a family or unexpected guests need not be a headache.

You can at all times concentrate only on 'best buys'. If, for instance, one particular week poultry is cheap, buy enough to make a dozen portions. Cook and freeze and you will have in store two meals for six people, three meals for four people, six meals for two people, etc.

You can vary the dish by using different sauces and you can freeze food in individual portions, in case you want to extract from your freezer a serving for one person.

You can plan whole meals and, if you have to be away, you will have the comfort of knowing that your family will enjoy a delicious home-cooked meal – all they will have to do will be to thaw and heat the food.

The freezer is a great boon to overworked mothers of big families, to professional people, the elderly and young working couples. It enables them to reduce drastically the time and energy spent on shopping. By keeping the freezer stocked with prepared dishes, meals can be produced in a matter of minutes.

Elderly people living in the country, or a mother with a young child, or any one of us, may not relish the idea of turning out of the house to go shopping when the weather is unpleasant. The freezer can be the answer to all such emergencies.

For those who live at some distance from the shops, there is another consideration: if you don't take a bus or drive your car to the shops every day, you will save the money that would go on fares or petrol.

And what about having to organize a big family reunion, a Christmas party, or any kind of entertaining at home? There is no need to knock yourself out on the day. You can plan and prepare all the food in advance, in easy stages, and have it ready in the freezer – including hors d'œuvres, roast bird to be served cold or hot, stuffing, bread, cakes, puddings, pies, etc.

I love cooking and never think of it as a chore, but who says it has to be done twice a day, every day? There is no reason why we shouldn't take days off. We should be free to pick and choose the time which is most convenient to us. People use their energy more creatively and successfully in the kitchen when they are not harassed by routine.

At the end of this section you will find a variety of recipes for dishes suitable for freezing, which will enable you to cater, with the minimum of trouble, for a small or large number of people.

How to choose a freezer
In considering the choice of an important piece of equipment, two questions arise immediately: (1) How much will it cost? (2) How much space will it occupy?

To take them in reverse order, space need not be a problem. There is on the market at least one small model which can fit on top of an existing refrigerator but, of course, the function it can perform is limited.

There are also refrigerators with separate frozen-food storage compartments. Most models with two separate doors offer the facility of freezing small quantities of fresh food. A popular size gives about 1 cubic foot (0·03 cubic metre) of frozen food storage mounted above a 5 cu ft (0·14 m³) refrigerator and this occupies very little more floor space than the average refrigerator.

Food freezers range in size from 2 cu ft up to over 20 cu ft (0·05–0·5 m³). Few of the popular cabinets are less than 24 in. (0·6 metre) in depth, so the variations are in width and height. The space inside a chest freezer is more versatile for odd-shaped packages than the shelves of an upright freezer which usually leave a certain amount of unpacked space at the top of each one. On the other hand, upright freezers are much easier to pack and unpack, and there is little difference in running cost between the two types.

If you have only limited space, you might care to consider other smaller 4 and 5 cu ft (0·11–0·14 m³) food freezers with front-opening doors. Some of these stack with their makers' matching refrigerators.

A very important new symbol was introduced after a meeting of the International Standards Organization in Paris. It is intended to supplement the existing star classification system for the storage of commercially frozen foods.

This new symbol is a large six-pointed star enclosed in a rectangular frame, together with the three-star symbol for frozen food storage with which we are all familiar. This symbol has been incorporated in a British Standard and we shall therefore see the large six-pointed star permanently and clearly featured on freezers. It is this symbol which clearly shows whether the appliance is designed merely for the storage of commercially frozen food or for freezing fresh food and storing it – as are freezers bearing the new symbol.

Freezer manufacturers are obliged to indicate the weight of food which can be frozen daily without causing any deterioration of the food already frozen.

This is where the fast-freeze switch serves its purpose. As you put in fresh batches of food, the special control overrides the thermostat and enables the temperature to go on dropping, so that your new batch of food can be frozen solid, without raising the temperature of the food stored in the freezer.

Your manual will tell you how long in advance this control should be set, but usually you may need from 2 to 5 hours. As soon as all the packs you have put in are frozen solid, the control should be switched back to normal. The amount of electricity required for the operation of the fast-freeze control is so small as to be insignificant, so don't worry about it causing your electricity bill to shoot up. It is included in the overall estimation of annual running cost of 1 unit per cubic foot per week (or in metric terms, a weekly consumption of 1 kilowatt-hour for each 0·03 m³ capacity).

The most uneconomical thing you can do is to keep the freezer empty or with very little food in it, because then you are wasting energy to cool the empty space. The freezer functions more efficiently when it is at least three-quarters full, because a good supply of food packages frozen solid provides its own insulation and helps to keep the temperature steady. Your freezer may have to be housed in a seemingly odd place, if your home is a bed-sitter or small flat. But be reassured that the kitchen is not always the best place for it, anyhow. It prefers a cool, dry atmosphere, so a boxroom or corridor may offer a site, or even a cupboard, or the space under the stairs, provided there is adequate ventilation. The weekly running cost is about 2p for each cubic foot (0·03 m³) and there is no significant difference between the chest and upright models. As mentioned, it is economical to keep the freezer about three-quarters full, but space should always be left for some fresh food to be put in. Most foods may be frozen, but the results will be better in some cases than in others. Provided the food is in good condition when it is put in the freezer, there will be no health risk if stored too long. But with some foods quality may suffer.

Food freezing is affected by personal choice: try freezing a small quantity of favourite foods to see if you and your family like the results before freezing large quantities.

All freezers have a fast freezing switch and most have a fast freezing area for freezing fresh food. How long food should be left in this section depends on the size, shape, and number of packets; density and sugar content of food; and how close the packets are to the freezing surface. It does not matter how long the food is left in this zone, but if you are freezing a considerable amount of food regularly – say, during the soft fruit season – then you need to move the food and stack it as soon as possible to make room for the next batch. It is best to leave each lot until the packets are frozen solid, usually overnight, then stack the packets in the storage zone. Return the fast-freeze switch to normal after all the fresh food has been frozen.

It is important to remember never to disconnect the freezer circuit. The safest way is to replace the socket outlet with a cover plate which has a 13 A cartridge fuse carrier and the flex connected permanently. Then nobody can accidentally unplug it. Get the electrician to fit the type with a red neon indicator so you can see it is in use. Never switch off this circuit at the mains. If it is your habit to turn everything off when you go on holiday, then do so by removing the fuses – except for the freezer circuit – rather than switching off the main switch.

If you get an interruption in supply, do not open the cabinet unless it is essential. The contents will be safe for at least 8 hours, but do not introduce fresh food for freezing during this period.

People who own and use freezers sensibly, invariably

say that they wish they had one of a bigger capacity. Unless space is desperately short or practically non-existent, don't automatically plump for the smallest model. Don't think of a freezer as an extravagance. It is a great time, labour, and money saver – an investment, a piece of invaluable, versatile equipment which will eventually pay for itself.

You have to decide for what purpose you are buying the freezer. Obviously, if you plan to freeze vast amounts of your own fruit, vegetables or other produce, you will need a larger model. The same applies if you mean to go in for bulk buying or wish to cater for a great deal of entertaining. Will you shop once a week, once a fortnight, or once a month? Have you a family and children for whom you want to provide ample ready-made meals in the school holidays, without slaving over a hot stove for hours every day? Do you want to store fresh bread and cakes? Both keep well in the freezer, and you won't need to bake more than once a month – but they need space. All these factors have a bearing on the size of the freezer which is best for your needs.

The above is only an outline of what is available. Almost anything one can say more precisely about technical details is likely to go out of date, as new models are constantly brought out.

If you contemplate buying a freezer, consider all the factors outlined above, weigh up the advantages and drawbacks of the basic types discussed, examine them and actually handle the models. Try out the chest type and the upright front-opening models. I am 5 ft 2 in. and have difficulty in reaching the bottom back portion of the chest-type freezer, so that's one of the snags to look out for. Also make sure that you have no problem in getting at the back of the top shelf of the upright model. Remember that you are buying a piece of equipment on which your household will rely for at least 10 years.

For further information on food freezers, call at your Electricity Board shop and discuss your needs with the staff who will be able to advise about both the best freezer for you and its installation.

Installation

Don't entrust the important job of installation to an amateur electrician. Go to the Electricity Board and get a qualified electrician to advise you where to install the freezer. The site is of paramount importance: it has to be cool, dry, and well ventilated. The freezer must be perfectly level to make sure that doors or lids – depending on the type of freezer you have chosen – close evenly on the seal.

The expert will almost certainly advise you to install the freezer on a separate circuit so as to permit the rest of the current to be switched off at times when your whole family may be away. Don't use a lighting socket.

Read carefully the manufacturer's instructions which come with the freezer and note all details on control settings, and so on.

To prepare the freezer for use, wash with plain warm water, without any detergent or soap. Dry well.

Don't touch the thermostat, which is normally pre-set, unless the instructions indicate some adjustment after washing. Switch on, leave to chill for 12 hours, or as set out in the instructions, and your new freezer is ready for use. As a precaution, unless you have a special cover plate, cover the socket outlet with adhesive tape to make sure that the current is not switched off by accident.

How to keep your freezer trouble-free
Most freezers carry a year's guarantee for the cabinet. If you follow the simple rules for food freezing, you should have no problems.

The worst thing that you can do is to disregard the repeated advice never to put warm, let alone hot, food into a freezer. By putting warm food into a freezer you at once cause twofold damage: you will cause excessive frost formation and you will bring about a deterioration in the quality of food already in the freezer. Frost formation may also be caused by overloading the capacity of the cabinet, so avoid excessive loads. A few reasonable-sized packages at a time are safer than one huge one. Be guided by the manufacturer's instructions.

Chest-type freezers need to be defrosted only once or twice a year; upright freezers, two or three times a year. The best time to defrost is when supplies are low. Several hours before defrosting, put lots of newspapers and a clean blanket in the freezer. These, when chilled, will serve to protect packets of frozen food.

Switch off the current, remove all packages, wrap in prepared newspapers (using several thicknesses), cover with the chilled blanket.

Leave the freezer open, to allow warm air to circulate. Place bowls of hot water inside it, to speed up the thawing, replacing the water if it gets cold. As soon as the ice has loosened from the sides, carefully scrape it off with a blunt wooden or plastic spatula. Never use any sharp or metal instrument.

Put a sheet of plastic foam or clean, old towels on the bottom of the freezer to catch the frost deposit and to make the task of removing it easier.

Wash with some bicarbonate of soda diluted in warm water. Allow 1 tablespoon of bicarbonate to a bowl of water. Never use any detergents or soap for cleaning the inside of the cabinet, or you may contaminate the food with their smell.

Make sure the cabinet is absolutely dry, close lid or door, switch on the current. The packets of food may be put back into the freezer straight away.

This is a good moment to check your stocks and make a note of what needs replacing. Also to clean the outside surfaces, as specified in manufacturer's instructions.

If the freezer stops working, first check your wiring, plugs, and fuses. This makes sure that the mains supply is still on, that the freezer is plugged in and the switch is on, and that a fuse has not blown. Then, if this is not the trouble, telephone the Electricity Board or the manufacturer's service department. Do not open the door of the freezer and keep the room cool and well ventilated.

If the engineer who comes to service the cabinet needs it to be emptied, remove, wrap, and store the packets of food as during defrosting, keeping them as cold as possible. The food should come to no harm for a couple of hours, but check all parcels for any signs of thawing. Do not freeze food that has been thawed – use it at once. Do not open the freezer lid or door for an hour or two after the current has been restored.

It is possible to insure against loss of contents of the freezer and most members of the British Insurance Association provide this facility.

Bulk buying

I have already referred to the facilities offered by some firms, who both deliver and sell frozen foods on the 'cash and carry' basis. As with choosing a freezer, here again it is a matter of assessing the best buy. Shop around, compare their ranges and price lists.

If you are buying food from a retail shop to keep in your freezer, insist on packages from below marked load lines. Examine the packages and firmly reject any which show signs of damaged packing. In a supermarket, always leave the buying of frozen food till last and ask for it to be well wrapped to insulate against thawing on the way home. Several layers of newspaper are useful for this purpose. Get your frozen-food supplies into your freezer with all possible speed. If you leave a small package of frozen food in a closed-up car parked in the sun, you may find it going limp. There is no way of rescuing it then for storage and the only thing to do is to cook and eat it as soon as possible.

In principle, the bigger the quantity of frozen food, the less it is likely to thaw on the way home, provided it is tightly packed and well wrapped.

What frozen foods to buy?
Deciding what to buy is a matter of individual taste and requirements. In the poultry line, you can buy whole turkeys, chickens, and ducks. You can also buy pieces of poultry, which are useful for an emergency

soup or casserole. Whole joints and smaller cuts of meat are available, as well as a choice of meat products, such as beefburgers, which are good value and can be cooked in a few minutes.

A lot of the fish is sold in fillet and portion packs, and some of the products are so well known I needn't mention them. Perhaps the greatest boon is frozen vegetables. Of course, there is nothing better than vegetables fresh from the garden, but what percentage of town dwellers can get them? Some vegetables, peas for instance, are at their best picked, say, an hour before serving. But if they've been lying around at the greengrocers for several days and spent a couple of days in transit, then their flavour and texture will not be nearly so good as those of quick-frozen peas. The same applies to corn on the cob.

There are some very good ice-creams, water ices, and similar preparations. If you buy these, pack them between packages of other frozen foods, to prevent thawing on the way home, though needless to say, I hope you will experiment with the recipes in this book and make your own.

Great quantities of prepared dishes are made and sold, but I hope that, in the main, my readers' freezers will be stocked with delicious dishes, lovingly made by their own hands.

Storage life of frozen food
Obviously everyone wants to know how long food can be stored in a freezer. Provided only really fresh produce is used and all the rules have been observed, food can keep indefinitely at 0 °F (-18 °C), but the eating qualities will start deteriorating.

As a rough guide, the storage life of various foods is set out below.

Raw Vegetables
Asparagus, beans, broccoli, sprouts, corn on the cob, mushrooms, parsnips, peas, peppers, spinach, turnips
9–12 months
Beetroot, carrots, cauliflower, leeks   6 months

New potatoes lose a certain amount of their texture and I personally wouldn't freeze them, but they are acceptable to most people. I'd rather enjoy the treat when they are at their best. Take small, whole new potatoes and cook almost completely. Cool quickly and freeze. Thaw by cooking 5 minutes in boiling salted water, drain, and serve with melted butter and chopped parsley.

Onions can be frozen and will keep for a couple of months, but they do go limp immediately, so it would hardly seem worth while freezing them.

Fruit
Apples, apricots, blackberries, blackcurrants, cherries, cranberries, gooseberries, grapefruit, lemons, loganberries, melon, oranges, peaches, pineapple, plums, raspberries, redcurrants, strawberries
9–12 months

Most fruits, except avocado, bananas, and pears, are suitable for freezing, and fortunately soft fruit, such as currants and raspberries, which are in season for a short time, freeze and keep well. Select sound fruit only, wash, stone, and prepare as for serving. Fruit can be frozen in dry sugar or in syrup.

Fish

White fish: cod, plaice, sole, haddock	6 months
Oily fish: halibut, salmon, trout	3–4 months
Shellfish (cooked)	2–3 months
Prawns and shrimps (cooked)	1–2 months
Prawns and shrimps (uncooked)	2–3 months

Meat

Large cuts of beef or lamb or venison will keep	10–12 months
Small cuts	6–8 months
Pork and veal – large cuts	4–5 months
Pork and veal – small cuts	3 months
Offal	2–3 months
Mince and sausages	1–2 months
Ham	3–4 months
Bacon	2 months

More than any other product meat requires careful wrapping to prevent drying, or 'freezer burn'. Study the section on wrapping and packing.

Poultry and game

Chicken	9–12 months
Duck, goose, turkey	5–6 months
Giblets	2–3 months
Game birds	6–8 months
Ground game	4–6 months

Only good-quality young poultry is suitable for freezing, either whole or jointed.

To freeze, prepare as for cooking, clean, truss, etc. Hang game before freezing.

Dairy produce

Butter (salted)	3 months
Butter (unsalted)	6 months
Soft cheese	4 months
Hard cheese	6 months
Cream (if pasteurized and at least 40% fat content)	3 months
Home-made ice-cream	3 months

Camembert, Brie, and similar soft cheeses, may be frozen when just ready for eating. They are not success-ful when kept in a refrigerator, but they may be frozen.

Eggs

I don't advise freezing eggs at all. You can't freeze whole raw eggs, because the shells will crack and this will make the yolks as tough as old plastic. If you freeze cooked eggs, the white will become as tough as old plastic. So you can't win. And, with eggs being so easily available, what is the point?

If for some reason, as an emergency, you need to freeze eggs for a short time, break four to six into a container, add a pinch of salt or a pinch of sugar, depending for what dish the eggs are intended, and mix lightly. Be sure to mark the containers clearly, so you won't use a salted egg for a dessert soufflé. In a similar way, you can freeze yolks and whites separately, but only, as I said, if it is absolutely unavoidable.

Other foods

Baked goods	1–2 months
Uncooked pastry	2–3 months
Soups, stock, and sauces	2–3 months
Stews, casseroles and curry dishes	2–3 months
Cooked, roast meat or poultry up to	2 months
Fish dishes	2–3 months
Pies	2–3 months
Desserts: soufflés, mousses, fruit flans, baked and steamed puddings	5–6 months
Bread and cakes	5–6 months

Basic foods for the freezer

From the information on storage life given in this chapter and the recipes in this book, you can compile your own list of desirable items for your freezer. Here is such a list of useful basic foods.

Vegetables

Peas, green beans, mixed vegetables, broccoli, spinach, carrots, Brussels sprouts, asparagus spears.

Cooked rice for savoury dishes and quick suppers.

Chopped parsley, mint, sage, chives, etc., wrapped in foil in small quantities.

Meats

Steaks, chops, joints, escalopes, sausages, chicken portions, steakburgers in small quantities.

Fish

Cod/haddock portions, buttered crumbed fish fillets, peeled prawns, home-made fish cakes, fish fingers.

Baked Goods

Sliced loaf for toasting, bread and rolls, unfilled Victoria sandwiches, fresh breadcrumbs, crumpets and scones, gâteaux.

Prepared Dishes

Individual meals such as roast lamb and vegetables, mixed grill with mushrooms, on aluminium foil plates and wrapped in foil. Portions of pâté. Portions of curry sauce; white or Bolognese sauce. Supplies of pastry and cooked flan cases. Casseroles. Unbaked sausage rolls and mince pies.

Fruit

Apples, blackberries, whole lemons, raspberries and sliced strawberries (in dry sugar), grated lemon and orange rind, lemon juice, apple sauce, and various fruit purées. Concentrated orange and grapefruit juice.

Miscellaneous

Ice cubes, fruit lollies, and sorbets; tomato purée, stock cubes, clear soups; uncooked individual Yorkshire puddings.

Items Not for Freezing

Bear in mind that some foods, fortunately not many, are not suitable for freezing. I have already explained why it is not advisable to freeze eggs. For the same reasons the same applies to real mayonnaise and egg custards.

Raw salad vegetables; celery, lettuce, cucumber, tomatoes are also not satisfactory, because they contain too much water.

According to experts, ordinary milk does not freeze well. This puzzles me, because I spent some of my student years in near-polar regions where it was too cold to put milk into bottles. The Laplanders used to bring the milk to the market and sell it frozen hard. The shape of these slabs of 'milk ice' was always round, like a Brie cheese but double the thickness, with a hole in the middle. If you bought a small amount, the vendor would chip it off with a chisel. If you went the whole hog and bought a complete 3-quart (3-litre) ring, you could carry it home threaded on a stout cord, like a huge white bead.

However, it is not recommended to freeze ordinary milk. You can, for emergencies, keep a quart (litre) of homogenized milk in the freezer.

Last but not least among things not to be kept in the freezer are carbonated drinks of all kinds. They have been known to go off with a terrible bang.

Packing materials
Headspace, sealing, and labelling
Having gone to the trouble and expense of installing a freezer and having prepared the supplies to put in it for storage, it would be a crime to sabotage your efforts by taking short cuts in packaging.

You must have packing materials which will effectively prevent dehydration and therefore loss of flavour and texture of your food. These must be moisture- and vapour-proof, otherwise 'freezer burn' may develop. Boxes and tub cartons must be waxed and these can be used again. Rubber bands or ordinary adhesive tape will not stand up to low temperatures, so please use the special adhesive tape recommended for sealing packages, to make airtight seals.

Packing materials must be odourless and strong enough both to withstand handling and to prevent flavours passing from one container to another. It would be fatal to allow your delicate lemon mousse to pick up the flavour of fish cakes.

All wrapping material should fit tightly around the food, to expel as much air as possible before sealing. Packing materials may be obtained either from the supplier of your home freezer, from large stationery shops, or from many department stores. Some firms also offer a selection of assorted materials for beginners. Most of the items are re-usable.

Packing materials
Listed below are some of the things you will find useful but you are unlikely to need them all: the basic equipment is polythene bags and plastic boxes with lids.

Polythene Bags
Excellent for all foods, except liquids. May be used on their own and moulded tightly round such irregular shapes as chickens and cuts of meat to exclude air, or they may be used as liners for cartons, to make for easy removal of food. Always use the thick polythene bags made for the purpose, which are obtainable in a wide variety of sizes.

Seals for Polythene Bags
Plastic or paper-coated wire ties ('Tite-ties') should be used for closing the bags, as these may be loosened without harming the bags.

Plastic Boxes
Small rigid or flexible containers with well-fitting lids of various sizes for liquids, fruit, vegetables, cooked foods, sauces.

Polytape
Special adhesive tape for sealing edges of boxes and for keeping packages secure. Also useful for holding labels.

Overwraps for Polythene Bags
It is a good idea to overwrap the bags containing large items with waxed brown paper, ordinary brown paper or mutton cloth. Heavy plastic-lined paper bags are sold in different colours for easy identification of different foods. Ordinary clean cardboard boxes of suitable sizes may also be used. This prevents damage to the polythene bags which might result in the food leaking and spoiling.

Plastic Sheeting by the Roll
This may be used to wrap joints, poultry, baked goods, and larger items. The sheeting is cut and sealed with the special adhesive tape. Rolls of very thin self-adhesive plastic film are available and this is suitable for wrap-

ping giblets of poultry, or small individual items which
are part of a larger pack.

Foil
Aluminium foil may be used for wrapping small quantities of food or for extra protection of food such as
chicken, but it is not suitable for acid fruit. As it may
puncture, it is still advisable to overwrap with polythene. The heavy-duty aluminium foil is, however,
more robust and therefore makes a very good external
wrap without additional covering.

Foil may be used for lining casseroles in which
stews for freezing are to be cooked. Then the food may
be frozen in the dish, and once frozen the foil-wrapped
food should be removed from the dish and over-
wrapped for storage. For reheating, the foil-wrapped
food should be returned to the same dish and the foil
removed just before serving.

Shaped Aluminium Foil Dishes
Useful for freezing pies, puddings, cakes, and individual
meals. Light, space-saving, and re-usable. The contents
should be covered with foil, and the whole dish enclosed in a plastic bag. Some types have their own foil
lids and need not be wrapped.

Underwraps
Chops or other small pieces of meat should be separated
with two layers or one fold of greaseproof paper, foil
or plastic. Wrap sharp edges – such as chicken legs –
in several thicknesses of thin polythene or foil to prevent
damage to outer wrap.

Headspace
Liquids will expand as they freeze, as will foods with a
lot of liquid in them, such as stews with gravies and
fruits in liquid. These foods should be frozen in a rigid
container filled almost to the top. A headspace of $\frac{1}{2}$–
$1\frac{1}{2}$ in. (up to about 4 cm) is usually enough, except with
big quantities.

Light-coloured fruit in syrup must be held under the
surface of the liquid to prevent discoloration. This may
be done by packing crumpled waxed or greaseproof
paper over the fruit up to the level of the lid.

Sealing
No sealing is necessary when a close-fitting snap plastic

lid is used on a polythene container. Polytape can be used to seal less well-fitting lids.

When using polythene bags moulded over irregularly shaped foods, space may be saved by standing the bags inside rectangular boxes, such as sugar boxes, while freezing takes place, so that a neat rectangular shape is achieved.

When the air has been removed, twist the neck of the bag tightly and fold it back on itself, securing it with a plastic or paper-covered wire tie. Twist the ends of the wire tightly together and thread one end through a small cardboard label. Secure by turning the ends of wire back on themselves.

You can heat-seal by using the edge of an electric iron at coolest setting, protecting the plastic from the direct heat with two pieces of tissue paper. Make the seal near the top of the bag so it may be cut off with the minimum of waste and the bag used again. An electric heat-sealer for bags is useful if you have large quantities of food to freeze at a time.

Labelling
Self-adhesive freezer-proof labels are very useful and may be used on all surfaces. Polythene packs can also be marked with a wax pencil.

Labels should give: kind of food and variety; quantity/weight; date; any specific information about future use.

It is often helpful to use different-coloured labels for different groups of food, say, red for meat, and green for vegetables. Alternatively, packets of similar food may be stored in nylon shopping bags of different colours.

Use a wax crayon, ballpoint or pencil for writing, as ink will run. If you have a large freezer, it is a good idea to keep a simple 'in-and-out' record of food frozen in order to use packs in correct rotation and to get an indication of quantities required by one's family through the year.

Preparing food for freezing
Anyone who has ever cooked a meal can freeze food successfully by following simple, common-sense rules.

All food has to be prepared as for cooking, i.e. cleaned, podded, peeled, cored, sliced, etc.

Freeze only small quantities at a time to prevent too great a rise in temperature in the freezer.

All vegetables must be blanched, i.e. scalded in

boiling water for a few minutes to stop the growth of
enzymes and ensure storage qualities. This is best done
in a large saucepan with a wire basket or stockinet bag.
Have 4 quarts (4 litres) of water boiling in the pan.
Blanch no more than 1 lb (500 g) of vegetables at a time,
so that boiling can be re-established quickly. Have a
large bowl of iced water standing by, with a supply of
ice cubes which can be added to keep the water
thoroughly chilled.

Plunge the wire basket with the 1 lb of prepared
vegetables into boiling water; as soon as it comes to the
boil again start calculating blanching time (*see timetable
overleaf*). Remove and plunge into iced water for the
same period.

Drain, pack into cartons or polythene bags, seal,
label, and freeze.

Timetable for blanching and cooling vegetables for freezing
Allow the same time for keeping in iced water as for
blanching in boiling water.

Artichokes	7 minutes
Asparagus	2–4 minutes depending on thickness
Aubergines (sliced)	4 minutes
Beans (broad)	3 minutes
Beans, French, whole	4 minutes
Beans, French, sliced	2 minutes
Beetroot	no blanching; cook until tender, then peel
Broccoli	3–4 minutes depending on thickness
Cabbage, in wedges (do not freeze for serving raw)	2–3 minutes
Carrots, small, whole	5 minutes
Cauliflower (in flowerets)	3 minutes
Celery, in 3 in. (8 cm) stalks (do not freeze for serving raw)	3 minutes
Corn on the cob	5–7 minutes according to size
Corn kernels	4 minutes
Parsnips, in wedges or slices	3 minutes
Peas	1 minute
Peppers, red and green	2 minutes
Spinach	2 minutes
Sprouts	3 minutes
Turnips, cubed	3 minutes

Methods of freezing fruit

Most fruit, correctly frozen, will keep for up to 12
months. Choose fruit in perfect condition, discarding
any which is soft or shows signs of over-ripeness.

Fruit can be frozen in unsweetened dry packs, in
sugar or in syrup.

Not all fruit lends itself to successful freezing. Peaches,
pears, apricots, and apples, for example, turn dark very
easily. To prevent discoloration, either dip these in
ascorbic acid solution, then dry pack, or add this
solution to syrup. Ascorbic acid tablets can be bought

from the chemist and the solution can be made by adding a 500 mg tablet to 1 pint ($\frac{1}{2}$ litre) of cold water.

Prepare fruit as for eating, wash if necessary, and keep in the refrigerator until ready to freeze. Avoid wetting soft fruit. Use small containers for easy planning.

Unsweetened dry packs
Freeze fruit on trays, then put into tubs, boxes, or bags. Seal, label, and freeze.

Dry sugar packs
This is particularly suitable for strawberries and other soft fruit. Allow 4 oz sugar to each pound of fruit (200 g per kilogram). Pack fruit in bags or cartons in layers, sprinkling with sugar. Leave $\frac{1}{2}$ in. (1 cm) headspace. Seal, label, and freeze.

Syrup packs
The amount of sugar in the syrup varies according to how acid the fruit is, or how much of a sweet tooth you have.

For a thin 30% syrup allow 8 oz of sugar for 1 pint of water. For a medium 40% syrup allow 12 oz of sugar for 1 pint of water. For a heavy 50% syrup allow 16–18 oz or more of sugar for 1 pint of water. (In metric terms: for each $\frac{1}{2}$ litre of water allow 200 g for thin, 300 g for medium, or 500–550 g for heavy syrup.)

To make the syrup, dissolve the sugar in hot water, cool, and chill thoroughly before using. Allow $\frac{1}{3}$ pint of syrup to 1 lb of fruit (400 ml per kilogram). Make sure all the fruit is covered by the syrup. Leave $\frac{1}{2}$–1 in. headspace (1–2 cm); seal, label, and freeze.

Cooked fruit
Apples can be peeled, cored, sliced, steamed for 1 or 2 minutes, cooled quickly as described, and packed in dry sugar or in 40% syrup. Or fruit can be sliced into prepared 30%, 40%, or 50% syrup.

Apples can be made into a purée or apple sauce and frozen in small wax cartons to be used as required.

I have dealt with the general rules for preparing raw and cooked fruit for freezing. Here now is a chart giving at a glance description of the method, packaging, thawing, and use of various kinds of fruit. When packing fruit into cartons, plastic containers and freezer bags, be careful to leave $\frac{1}{2}$–1 in. (1–2 cm) headspace to allow for expansion during freezing.

For pies, thaw before cooking. To serve hot, simmer gently in the syrup. To serve cold, thaw unopened in the refrigerator and use at once.

To save monotony, I have not repeated the same details of the process of freezing each item. I emphasize that, whatever fruit or other food you are freezing, when packing in plastic bags, waxed cartons or other containers, you must leave from $\frac{1}{2}$ in. to 1 in. headspace (1–2 cm). This is space above the food, at the top of the container. It is essential to allow for expansion during freezing.

Having packed the food, the containers must be sealed and labelled. Then it is ready to be frozen.

	Method	Packing
Apples	See above	
Apricots	Stone and halve	Pack in plastic containers in 40% syrup
Bilberries	Stalk, wash, and dry	Pack in dry sugar in waxed cartons or plastic containers
Blackberries	Wash and dry	
Blackcurrants	As for bilberries	Pack in waxed cartons or plastic containers in dry sugar or 50% syrup
Cherries	Wash, dry, and stone	Pack in waxed cartons or plastic freezer bags
Cranberries	Wash and dry	Pack in waxed cartons or freezer bags, in dry sugar, or plain without sugar
Damsons	Wash and stone	As for greengages
Gooseberries	Top and tail, wash, leave whole	Pack in cartons or freezer bags, in dry sugar or 50% syrup
Grapefruit	Peel, remove pith and seeds, divide into segments. Or squeeze juice and add sugar to taste	Pack in waxed cartons or plastic containers in 30% syrup
Grapes	Wash, dry, remove seeds	Pack in waxed cartons or plastic containers, in dry sugar or 30% syrup

	Method	Packing
Greengages	Wash, halve, and stone	Pack in plastic containers or waxed cartons in 50% syrup
Lemons	Peel, remove pith and pips. Slice or squeeze out juice and add sugar to taste. Grated lemon rind can be frozen in small quantities for use as required	Pack in cartons in 30% syrup
Loganberries	Wash, if necessary, and dry	Pack in waxed cartons or plastic containers in dry sugar
Melon	Peel, seed, and slice or cube. Sprinkle with lemon juice	Pack as above, in dry sugar or 30% syrup
Oranges	As grapefruit	
Oranges for marmalade	Use whole Seville oranges. Wash	Freeze whole, each wrapped in self-adhesive plastic sheeting or polythene bags. Or slice and pack in measured quantities. When making marmalade from frozen oranges, to compensate for loss of pectin, allow 10% more fruit
Peaches	Dip in boiling water for 30 seconds. Cool in cold water and peel. Cut in half, remove stones. Freeze in halves or slice	Pack in waxed cartons, or plastic containers, in 40% syrup with ascorbic acid solution. Make sure fruit is submerged in syrup. If necessary, put crumpled waxed paper on top, to keep peaches covered with liquid. Thaw in unopened carton and use at once.
Pears	Peel, core, quarter, and sprinkle with lemon juice	Pack in plastic containers or waxed cartons, in 30% syrup with ascorbic acid solution
Pineapple	Peel, core, slice or cube	Pack as above, in 40% syrup
Plums	Wash, dry, halve, and stone	Pack as above in dry sugar or 50% syrup

	Method	*Packing*
Raspberries	Stem, wash if necessary, and dry	Pack as above in dry sugar
Redcurrants	As above	
Rhubarb	Choose young stalks. Wash, cut in 1 in. (2 cm) pieces. Blanch in boiling water for 1 minute. Cool	Pack in dry sugar or 50% syrup
Strawberries	Hull, wash if necessary, and dry	Pack in dry sugar

Recipes for the Freezer

Rillettes (French Pâté)

Dice the pork and put it into a heavy-bottomed saucepan with the cloves, salt, pepper, and bouquet garni. Pour over the cup of water. Cook over the lowest heat possible (the contents should barely tremble) for 5 hours. Stir every now and then to prevent the meat sticking to the pan. With a wooden spatula, squash the contents of the pan until they form a good amalgam. At this stage, you should not be able to distinguish a single lump of meat in your pâté. Let the pâté cook, at the same rate as before, for 15 minutes more. Remove from the heat and cool. Put into foil dishes, smooth top, cover with a layer of rendered fat, and seal with heavy foil and freeze.

Thaw at room temperature, turn out, cut into portions of required size, and serve with hot toast.

12–14 Servings
6 lb (3 kg) pork (belly of pork very suitable)
2 cloves
4 oz (100 g) sea salt
1 teaspoon pepper
bouquet garni
8 oz (200 ml) water
12 oz (300 g) rendered fat

Israeli Brain Pâté

Wash and blanch the brain (p. 169) and chop up. Chop the onion finely and fry gently in the olive oil taking care the onion does not go brown. Add parsley, garlic, salt and pepper, lemon juice, and water. When the liquid begins to boil, add the chopped brain and cook over medium heat until all the liquid has evaporated.

Remove the frying pan from the heat.

Beat the eggs as for an omelette. Add them to the brain mixture. Prepare a lightly buttered soufflé mould and into it pour the contents of the frying pan. Place the soufflé mould in a pan of water (bain-marie) and cook in a medium oven at 375 °F (190 °C) for 45 minutes.

This pâté can be served hot or cold.

Cool, put into foil dishes, smooth top, seal with heavy foil, and freeze.

Thaw at room temperature, turn out, cut into portions of required size, and serve with hot toast.

6 Servings
1 calf's brain
1 small onion
1 tablespoon olive oil
1 oz (25 g) chopped parsley
1 finely crushed clove garlic
salt
pepper
juice of 1 lemon
1 tablespoon water
5 eggs

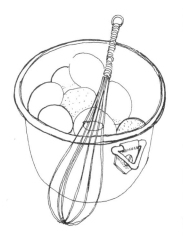

Stock

Good-quality stock can be kept in the freezer until required for making soup, and the more concentrated the stock the better. So for freezing boil it down to reduce and concentrate. Cool as quickly as possible and remove any surface fat. You can freeze stock in plastic containers, leaving a 1 in. (2 cm) headspace in a 1 pint (½ litre) container. Or, which is even more convenient, freeze it in ice-cube trays. You can then use the small amount of stock you may need for a sauce or gravy.

Thaw clear stocks over direct heat, or add cubes of stock to whatever you are cooking.

Chicken Carcass Stock
Put the chicken carcass and giblets, if any, in a pan, cover with cold water, bring to the boil, skim, season with salt and 2–3 peppercorns, simmer for 2–2½ hours, strain.

If the stock is not required for use immediately, leave to cool, then keep in a refrigerator. The fat will settle on the top and can easily be peeled off and used for cooking.

Giblet Stock
Whenever you are roasting a chicken, or any other bird, you are bound to need stock for the sauce or gravy. Therefore, as you remove or unpack the giblets, put them to cook straight away. Proceed as with any stock: put the giblets into a pan, cover with cold water, bring to the boil, skim, season, simmer for 1½–2 hours, depending on the age of the bird they came from, strain, allow to cool.

All cooking and freezing instructions given for chicken carcass or giblet stocks apply to stocks made of capon, duck, turkey, goose, or any game.

4 Servings
2 sets giblets cleaned and chopped
1 small chopped onion
1 diced carrot
small piece diced parsnip
2 peeled sliced tomatoes
2 tablespoons chicken fat
1 tablespoon flour
1 quart (1 litre) water or chicken-bone stock
salt and pepper
1 glass sherry
1 tablespoon chopped dill (or parsley)

Giblet Soup
Brown the giblets, except the liver, and the vegetables in chicken fat over low heat for 10–12 minutes. Dust with flour, blend it in, and cook gently for 2–3 minutes.

Gradually dilute with stock, bring to the boil, then simmer until the giblets are tender. At 2–3 minutes before the end of cooking add liver. Season to taste, sprinkle with dill, and serve.

To freeze, after seasoning, stand pan in bowl of iced water to cool quickly. Skim off fat which forms on the surface. Pour cold soup into plastic containers, leaving 1–1½ in. (up to 4 cm) headspace, seal, and freeze.

To serve, turn out frozen soup into a saucepan, gently bring to the boil. Check seasoning, add sherry, and sprinkle with dill.

Meat Borsch

This is a great soup and lends itself to freezing admirably. Traditionally, long before there was any refrigeration, it was considered a good idea to make double the amount of borsch needed, because it tastes even better the second time round.

Wash and dry the meat, trim off surplus fat, cut into pieces, and put in a saucepan with water. Bring to the boil, skim off any scum which rises to the surface, reduce heat, cover, and simmer for 45 minutes.

Reserve one beetroot. Shred the cabbage and cut all root vegetables first into slices, then into 'matchsticks'. Quarter the onion and slice thinly. Add all vegetables to stock and continue to simmer for 20–25 minutes. Add tomato purée, vinegar, sugar, bay leaf, salt, pepper, and allspice. Cook for 15 minutes on low heat.

Remove from heat, stand in a pan of iced water to cool quickly. Decant into rigid containers, leaving 1½ in. (4 cm) headspace, seal, and freeze. Before use, thaw, heat to boiling point, breaking up with a fork as the soup begins to thaw.

To ensure the characteristic attractive rich colour of borsch, keep one beetroot for last-minute use. Grate it finely, put in a small pan with a cupful of stock, simmer for 5 minutes, and strain into the borsch.

Check seasoning, sharpen with lemon juice, sprinkle with chopped dill and parsley, and serve with sour cream.

Serve meat or mushroom pirozhki (*see below*) separately.

8 Servings
1½ lb (750 g) stewing beef
2¼ quarts (2¼ litres) water
1 lb (½ kg) white cabbage
3–4 beetroots
2 carrots
1 parsnip
2 stalks celery
1 large onion
4 tablespoons tomato purée
1 tablespoon red wine vinegar
1 tablespoon sugar
1–2 bay leaves
1½ teaspoons salt
¼ teaspoon ground black pepper
4–5 whole allspice seeds
1 tablespoon lemon juice
1 tablespoon chopped dill
1 tablespoon chopped parsley
sour cream

Meat Pirozhki

Roll out pastry to a thickness of ¼ in. (½ cm) and cut into circles.

Make sure the filling is cold. Put a spoonful of filling on each circle of dough or pastry, fold over into semicircles, and pinch edges together. Whisk egg with salt and use the mixture for brushing the pirozhki, to give them a beautiful glaze.

Put the baking tray with the glazed pirozhki in a refrigerator for 30 minutes. Pre-heat oven to 450 °F (230 °C) and bake the pirozhki until golden.

Put in freezer paper, seal, and freeze. To use, thaw at room temperature, then heat in oven at 400 °F (200 °C) for 20–25 minutes.

6 Servings
puff pastry
beef filling (p. 142)
1 beaten egg for glazing
¼ teaspoon salt

6 Servings
1 lb (½ kg) fresh sliced mushrooms
½ teaspoon salt
¼ teaspoon pepper
3 tablespoons chopped spring onions
1 tablespoon dill or parsley
2 oz (50 g) butter
3 tablespoons sour cream
puff pastry
1 egg

Mushroom Pirozhki

Put the mushrooms in a saucepan, sprinkle with salt, pepper, spring onions, and dill. Stir and sweat them over low heat for a few minutes. As soon as the mushrooms yield up their juices, add butter and sour cream. Simmer gently for 10 minutes. Remove and chill before using the filling. Roll out and cut out pastry, fill and shape as described in preceding recipe for meat pirozhki. Beat egg with a pinch of salt, glaze the pirozhki, and place in refrigerator until ready to bake.

Heat oven to 450 °F (230 °C). Bake as described.

Put in freezer paper or polythene bag, seal, and freeze.

To use, thaw at room temperature, heat in the oven at 400 °F (200 °C) for 20–25 minutes.

Rolled Pancakes

These rolled pancakes can be served as an accompaniment to clear soups, or as a course in their own right. The filling can be varied: minced chicken, chicken livers, rice and mushrooms, salmon, veal, chopped hard-boiled eggs, spring onions, etc.

4 Servings
4 oz (100 g) self-raising flour
pinch salt
1 teaspoon sugar
1 lightly beaten egg
½ pint (250 ml) warm water
butter

For batter

Combine flour, salt, and sugar, stir in egg, and gradually blend in water. Mix well and leave for 25–30 minutes. Heat a frying pan, brush with butter, pour a small ladleful of batter into the pan, and tilt it to spread the batter evenly over the bottom. Do not pour in more than 2½ tablespoons at a time. If you put in too much, pour it off. Fry on one side only. As soon as one side is done, turn the pancake out on to a wooden board and cover with a cloth to keep warm. Grease the pan again and proceed to fry the rest of the pancakes.

For filling

Heat 2 tablespoons butter and fry onion until soft. Add beef and brown. Add mushrooms, cook together for 5 minutes, stirring all the time to prevent sticking and adding more fat if necessary.

2 tablespoons butter
1 small finely chopped onion
8 oz (200 g) fresh minced beef
2 tablespoons chopped mushrooms
1–2 chopped hard-boiled eggs
4 tablespoons stock or water
salt and pepper
½ tablespoon chopped dill or parsley
*a little white of egg for sealing pancake
    rolls*

Add eggs, stock, seasoning, and dill. Cook, stirring for 1–2 minutes, remove from heat.

Place the pancakes fried side up, put a spoonful of filling at one edge, fold it over, tuck in sides, and roll the pancakes. Brush the edge of the outer flap with egg white to prevent unrolling.

To freeze: wrap rolled filled pancakes, put in polythene bag, seal, and freeze.

Before use, thaw, fry to brown lightly on all sides and to heat thoroughly.

Béchamel Sauce

Melt the butter, add flour gradually, and cook this roux on a fairly low heat until it begins to come away from the pan, but on no account allow it to colour.

Little by little, add milk and seasoning, stirring constantly, to ensure a smooth and creamy texture.

To freeze: put the pan in a bowl of iced water and chill quickly, stirring from time to time.

Spoon cold sauce into suitable rigid container, leaving ½ in. (1 cm) headspace. Seal, label, and freeze.

To serve: heat frozen sauce in double saucepan until thawed. Beat well until smooth. Check seasoning, heat thoroughly and, if the sauce is too thick, blend in a little milk or stock.

2 oz (50 g) butter
2 oz (50 g) flour
½ pint (250 ml) hot milk
salt and pepper

Cheese Sauce

Make Béchamel sauce. Add 4 oz (100 g) grated cheese, then follow instructions for freezing, etc., as for Béchamel sauce.

Wiener Schnitzel

Cut veal into escalopes, flatten to make them very thin. Put a little flour in a paper bag, season with salt and pepper, and shake to mix well. Dip escalopes in seasoned flour, then in beaten egg, and finally in breadcrumbs, pressing well to make them adhere.

Heat fat and fry escalopes until golden on both sides.

Shell eggs and chop the whites and the yolks separately. Arrange schnitzels on a heated serving dish, top each with an olive wrapped in anchovy fillet. Garnish with egg whites and yolks in separate group. Put the lemon slices around the dish and serve.

For freezing, after frying the escalopes, drain on kitchen paper, cool quickly, pack into a suitable box, interleaving with cellophane paper if necessary, seal, and freeze.

Before using, unwrap, heat uncovered, then arrange on a dish, garnish, and serve as described.

6 Servings or 2 for 3 people
2 lb (1 kg) fillet of veal
flour
salt and pepper
2 beaten eggs
breadcrumbs
4 oz (100 g) butter or other fat
3 hard-boiled eggs
5–6 stoned olives
5–6 anchovy fillets
1 peeled, sliced lemon

Veal Ramekins with Brains

4–5 Servings
6 oz (150 g) calf's brain
vinegar
butter or margarine
1 finely chopped onion
12 oz (300 g) minced veal
½ tablespoon flour
½ pint (250 ml) stock or water
salt and pepper
juice of ½ lemon
¼ teaspoon grated lemon rind
4 oz (100 g) chopped mushrooms
3 eggs
1 tablespoon breadcrumbs

Soak the brains in cold water for 1 hour, remove skin and any traces of blood, bring to the boil in enough water to cover, with a dash of vinegar, for 10 minutes. Drain, plunge into cold water, allow to cool.

Heat 2 oz (50 g) butter or margarine, fry the onion until it becomes soft, add veal, and cook gently until tender. Sprinkle with flour, stir it in well, dilute with stock, and season. Leave simmering for 5 minutes.

Meanwhile, drain and dry the brains, slice, fry lightly in 1 tablespoon butter or margarine, and add to veal with lemon juice and rind. Toss the mushrooms in the butter left from frying the brains and add to the mixture. One by one, blend in eggs. Grease 4–5 ramekin dishes, divide the mixture between them, sprinkle with breadcrumbs, dot with tiny pieces of butter or margarine, put in a pre-heated oven at 425 °F (220 °C), bake for 10 minutes and serve.

For freezing, cool the mixture quickly, divide between 4–5 suitable containers, if you want to use only one or two portions at a time, or pack into a single big container. Leave a headspace, seal, and freeze in the usual way.

To serve, heat in a double boiler, then proceed to put in ramekin dishes and finish off as described.

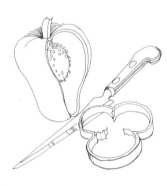

Navarin de Mouton

4 Servings
1½ lb (750 g) boned shoulder of lamb
3 tablespoons oil
pinch of sugar
salt, pepper
3 tablespoons flour
meat stock
1 bouquet garni
2 cloves garlic
2 dozen baby onions
1 oz (25 g) butter
1 lb (½ kg) potatoes (new ones look best)
8 oz (200 g) turnips
5 oz (125 g) baby carrots
8 small tomatoes

Cut the meat into 2 in. (5 cm) cubes. Put oil into a saucepan and add lamb, sugar, salt, and pepper. Sprinkle with flour and brown the meat, stirring constantly. Barely cover with stock. Add bouquet garni and the garlic crushed but not skinned. Bring to boiling point and lower heat to simmer.

Skin the baby onions and glaze in the butter. Peel the potatoes, turnips, and carrots (leave new potatoes and baby carrots whole or cut all roots into bite-sized pieces). When the lamb has simmered for 45 minutes, add all the vegetables. Prick the skin of the little tomatoes before adding to the dish, to stop them from bursting. Cover and simmer for an hour. Don't stir during cooking, but baste with the juice from time to time.

Lovely for winter. Reheats like a dream.

For freezing, cool quickly as described, decant into plastic container, leaving headspace, cover closely, seal, and freeze.

To serve, turn out into a saucepan, reheat gently, stirring from time to time.

Hungarian Goulash

Cut the beef and veal into 1 in. (2 cm) cubes. Heat the dripping, quickly brown the meat, add onions and garlic, and continue to brown. Transfer to a thick-bottomed saucepan, add tomatoes and green pepper, moisten with stock, cover, and simmer for 1 hour or more, till the meat begins to be tender. Add potatoes, season with salt and pepper to taste, heighten with paprika, add caraway seeds, cover, and continue to simmer until the potatoes are done.

Either serve at once piping hot, or freeze for use on another occasion.

To freeze, stand the pan in a bowl of iced water to cool as quickly as possible, stirring from time to time. You can freeze it in the same casserole. Remove from casserole when frozen, wrap, seal, and store in freezer. Or you can decant the goulash into two separate suitable plastic or foil containers leaving headspace, seal, and freeze.

8 Servings or 2 for 4 people
1 lb (½ kg) lean beef
¼ lb (200 g) lean veal
2 oz (50 g) dripping
2 medium-sized chopped onions
1 clove chopped garlic
¼ lb (200 g) peeled, sliced tomatoes
1 seeded, sliced green pepper
1 pint (½ litre) stock (or water with bouillon cube)
1 lb (½ kg) potatoes, cut in large dice
1 teaspoon salt
¼ teaspoon black pepper
1 dessertspoon paprika
small pinch caraway seeds

Poppy Seed Roll

Dough

Cream the yeast with half a tablespoon sugar in a basin or in a mixer. Warm the milk gently with the margarine until the margarine melts. Pour milk and margarine mixture on the yeast and blend well. Take care not to overheat the milk; it should be lukewarm.

Warm a mixing bowl big enough to take all dough ingredients and to allow for rising. Sift flour and salt into it, make a well in the centre and pour in the yeast and milk mixture. Work in the flour from the sides and knead until you get a smooth dough. Cover with a lightly floured cloth and leave to rise in a warm place until the dough doubles in bulk. This may take from 1½ to 2 hours. Sprinkle in remaining sugar and work in beaten eggs. Knead well and dough is ready for rolling out.

Filling

Prepare filling while the dough is rising, i.e. before you add sugar and eggs, to allow filling time to cool. Rinse the poppy seeds with hot water, drain well (this is best done in a muslin bag), grind finely.

Bring the milk to the boil gently, with honey and

1 oz (25 g) fresh yeast
3 oz (75 g) sugar
¼ pint (250 ml) milk
4 oz (100 g) melted margarine
1 lb (½ kg) flour
pinch salt
3 beaten eggs

12 oz (300 g) poppy seeds
¼ pint (250 ml) milk
3 tablespoons honey
2 tablespoons sugar
2 tablespoons chopped candied peel
¼ teaspoon vanilla flavouring
1 teaspoon powdered cinnamon
1 tablespoon melted margarine

sugar. Add poppy seeds, cook, stirring frequently, until the mixture becomes thick. Add candied peel, vanilla flavouring, and cinnamon, stir, and remove from heat. Leave to cool. Roll out the dough on a floured board into a rectangle $\frac{1}{4}$ in. ($\frac{1}{2}$ cm) thick. Moisten the edges and spread the filling thickly over the rectangle of dough almost to the edges. Roll up lightly and seal the edges. Put the roll in a baking tin, greased with melted margarine, cover with a cloth, and leave again in a warm place to rise for another $1\frac{1}{2}$ to 2 hours.

Pre-heat oven to 375 °F (190 °C). Brush the top of the poppy seed roll with melted margarine and bake for about 1 hour. If desired, mixed chopped dried fruit and/or chopped nuts may be added to the filling.

To freeze, chill unwrapped, then cover closely in freezer wrap and freeze. Thaw at room temperature in the wrapper.

Honey and Hazelnut Cake

6 Servings
a little butter
5 eggs
4 oz (100 g) honey
2 oz (50 g) ground hazelnuts
2 tablespoons sugar
3 oz (75 g) sifted cake flour
4 tablespoons double cream

Pre-heat oven to 300 °F (150 °C). Butter the cake tin. Separate eggs. Combine yolks with honey, stir with a wooden spoon to mix thoroughly, or put through a blender. Pound hazelnuts and sugar in a mortar or put through a grinder to reduce to powder. Little by little stir flour into the honey and yolk mixture. Equally gradually add hazelnuts, stir well. Blend in cream.

Beat the whites until stiff, fold into the cake mixture, gently lifting with a pallet knife as you mix.

Pour into prepared cake tin, bake 30 minutes. Cool before removing from tin.

For freezing, cool as quickly as possible and make sure the middle is cold, too. Freeze unwrapped on a tray, then envelop in freezer wrap and freeze.

To serve, thaw for 4–5 hours at room temperature.

Iced Walnut Gâteau

6 Servings
12 oz (300 g) walnuts
6 egg yolks
10 oz (250 g) sugar
1 teaspoon butter
6 stiffly beaten whites of egg
vanilla custard (p. 109)

Grind the nuts into coarse flour, mix three-quarters of it with egg yolks. Beat until the mixture is well blended. Add sugar and repeat beating to amalgamate the ingredients. Pre-heat oven to 400 °F (200 °C). Butter two layer cake tins. Fold stiffly beaten egg whites into the walnut mixture, lifting gently to keep it as light as possible. Divide the gâteau mixture equally between the two tins and bake for 30 minutes. Cool before removing from tins.

Mix reserved ground walnuts with vanilla custard to make filling. Spread filling on one of the cakes and set the other on top, to make a two-tier sandwich.

Freeze uncovered. Put in a polythene bag or box and mark it 'fragile' so that nothing heavy is put on top of the gâteau.

Thaw at room temperature.

Crêpes Suzette
Batter

Blend the milk and flour in a bowl with a whisk. Add egg yolks, stirring well until blended. Add sugar and stir again. Melt the butter in a double boiler and pour it into the mixture. Fold in the beaten egg whites and mix well.

10 Servings
¾ pint (375 ml) milk
10 oz (250 g) sifted flour
4 egg yolks
4 tablespoons sugar
8 oz (200 g) butter
4 egg whites beaten stiff

When the batter is ready, add 2 tablespoons brandy.

Cook 20 paper-thin pancakes.

Cool them on a rack, pack with cellophane between each pancake. Wrap in freezer paper or put in a polythene bag and freeze.

Before using, separate pancakes and leave on rack to thaw completely.

Butter a metal serving dish and heat it slightly. Spread the crêpes with the orange butter, fold in quarters, arrange on the dish, and heat through.

Heat 5 tablespoons brandy in a small pan and pour it over the crêpes. Ignite and serve at once.

brandy
orange butter (p. 61)

Grapefruit Mousse

Beat egg yolks with sugar until light and pale. Transfer to a double boiler, add fruit juices and heat over simmering water until the mixture becomes thick and creamy, stirring all the time.

Remove from heat and allow to cool.

Beat egg whites until very stiff, fold into the grapefruit mixture, pour into a serving dish, and chill.

To freeze, pour cooled mixture into a suitable plastic container, leave to set in refrigerator, seal, and freeze.

To serve, thaw overnight in refrigerator or for 2–3 hours at room temperature.

4 Servings
5 raw egg yolks
6 oz (150 g) sugar
juice of 1 grapefruit
2 tablespoons lemon juice
5 egg whites

1 pint (½ litre) double cream
*2 oz (50 g) vanilla-flavoured icing
    sugar*

Whipped Cream Rosettes

Whisk the cream until thick but light, fold in sugar.
Pipe rosettes on a tray and freeze.

Pack in layers in waxed or plastic container, putting sheets of cellophane between the layers. Store in freezer.

You can also freeze the whipped cream in a tub.

To serve, thaw in refrigerator.

GENERAL RECIPES

So far the recipes in this book have been chosen not only for their culinary interest, but because they can be easily prepared with the help of various electrical appliances.

I now want to introduce you to a general collection of recipes. All are favourites of mine and are chosen, not only for their simplicity and variety, but because they reflect the growing and very welcome trend towards a more international cuisine.

Starters and Fish Courses

Johnsson's Temptation

4 Servings
4 large raw potatoes
10–12 anchovies
1 tablespoon breadcrumbs
2 medium-sized finely chopped onions
4 oz (100 g) butter
freshly ground black pepper
½ pint (250 ml) single cream

Wash, peel, and shred the potatoes, or cut into thin straws. Cut anchovies into small pieces. Butter a baking dish, sprinkle with breadcrumbs. Put in potato, anchovies, and onion in alternate layers, ending with a layer of potatoes. Season with pepper to taste, dot with butter and put in a pre-heated oven at 400 °F (200 °C) for 10 minutes. Cover with cream and continue to bake in a moderate oven at 375 °F (190 °C) for 50–60 minutes, or until the potatoes are done and the top acquires a delicate brown colour.

Canadian Eggburgers

4 Servings
4 large round rolls
4 slices of cheese
1 tablespoon butter
4 eggs
salt and pepper
1 small onion, cut into rings

Split the rolls, put on a rack split side up, cover half of the splits with cheese slices cut to match (the other halves will be used as 'caps'). Put both cheese-covered and plain halves of rolls under the grill to melt the cheese and toast the rolls. Fry the eggs in butter, turn once, season to taste, and arrange on the cheese-covered halves. Top with onion rings, cover with 'caps', and serve with any piquant sauce, pickles or mustard.

Eggs Milanese

4 Servings
6 oz (150 g) spaghetti
salt and pepper
4 hard-boiled eggs
1 oz (25 g) butter or margarine
1 tablespoon finely chopped onion

Boil the spaghetti in plenty of salted water for 10 minutes, drain, and season. Keep hot. Cut the eggs into halves, remove yolks, purée in a blender with half the butter and onion until smooth, season with salt and pepper.

Fill the egg whites with the purée. Arrange stuffed eggs in an oven-proof dish, surrounded with spaghetti,

dot with remainder of butter in small pieces, put in a
hot oven at 425 °F (220 °C) or under a grill to brown
the tops of eggs, and serve.

Chinese Lobster Omelette

Dice the lobster meat. Heat oil, put in onion, and cook
gently for 30 seconds. Add lobster, cook for 2 minutes,
season with salt to taste. Pour on eggs, mix quickly,
cook for 1 minute, sprinkle with pepper. Shake the
pan carefully to ensure even cooking, cook for 1
minute, and serve at once.

6 Servings
8 oz (200 g) lobster meat
1 tablespoon oil
1 tablespoon chopped onion
salt
6 beaten eggs
pinch fresh ground pepper

Pacific Prawns with Lettuce

Peel prawns (Dublin Bay or the large Pacific kind are
best for this dish), leaving tail tips on. Split lengthwise
and remove intestinal cord. Put prawns on a plate,
sprinkle with a pinch of salt, ginger, and cornflour.
Shred lettuce coarsely. Heat oil in a pan with garlic,
add prawns, and sauté briskly. As soon as the prawns
change colour, add lettuce. Cook for 1 minute, season
with pepper, add more salt if necessary, pour in water,
bring to the boil, stir, and serve.

4 Servings
1 lb (⅓ kg) large raw prawns
salt
2–3 slices pounded ginger
2 teaspoons cornflour
1 crisp washed lettuce
1 tablespoon oil
1 crushed clove garlic
freshly ground pepper
4 oz (100 ml) water

Salmon Cream in Aspic

Poach fresh salmon, allow to cool, flake with a fork,
remove all skin and bones. (If tinned salmon is used,
drain off all liquid.) Cream salmon with butter by
hand, or in a blender, season to taste. Whisk the cream
until stiff and fold into the salmon mixture. Dissolve
gelatine in cold water, add boiling water, stir, and
leave to cool and thicken slightly. Line a mould with
half-set jelly. To do this, pour a layer of jelly on one
side of the mould at a time and put in a refrigerator to
set. Proceed in this manner until all sides and bottom
have a coating of jelly.

4–6 Servings
1 lb (⅓ kg) fresh or tinned salmon
3 oz (75 g) butter
salt and pepper
4 oz (100 ml) cream
2 tablespoons plain gelatine
4 tablespoons cold water
4 oz (100 ml) boiling water

Fill the mould with salmon cream, seal the top with
jelly, chill until it sets.

To serve, turn out the mould on to a dish.

Herring in Oatmeal

4 Servings
4 plump filleted fresh herrings
salt and pepper
milk
fine oatmeal
fat for deep frying
lemon

Season the herrings, dip in milk, coat with oatmeal, and deep fry in hot fat until golden-brown. Drain, garnish with lemon wedges, and serve.

Chilean Turbot with Avocado Dressing

4 Servings
1½ lb (750 g) turbot
court-bouillon (p. 180)
1–2 avocado pears, depending on size
juice of ¼ lemon
salt and pepper
pinch cayenne pepper
3–4 tablespoons single cream

Poach the turbot in a court-bouillon. Drain, allow to cool, arrange on a serving dish. Just before serving, mash the flesh of an avocado pear with lemon juice, season to taste, thin down with cream to desired consistency, and mask the turbot with this dressing.

Turbot au Gratin

4 Servings
4 portions of turbot fillet
salt and pepper
4 tablespoons melted butter
4 tablespoons dry vermouth
sifted breadcrumbs
2 oz (50 g) grated Parmesan cheese

Season the fish with salt and pepper, brush with butter, sprinkle with vermouth. Grill, allowing 3 minutes for each side and basting two or three times with butter and vermouth. Mix breadcrumbs with cheese, sprinkle turbot portions with the mixture, return to grill, cook for one more minute each side, and serve.

Florentine Prawn and Cheese Soufflé

4–6 Servings
butter
4 oz (100 g) grated Parmesan cheese
½ pint (250 ml) thick white sauce
  (p. 178)
salt and cayenne pepper
4 raw egg yolks
3 tablespoons prawn butter (p. 178)
4 tablespoons cream
6 stiffly beaten egg whites
8 oz (200 g) peeled prawns

Pre-heat oven to 375 °F (190 °C). Butter a soufflé mould. Add cheese to white sauce, season. One by one blend in egg yolks. Mix prawn butter with cream and stir into sauce. Fold in egg whites.

Pour a layer of the mixture into the soufflé dish, scatter with prawns, and continue in this manner until all are used up. Bake for 35 minutes.

Whiting Orly

4 Servings
8 fillets of whiting
juice of ¼ lemon
2 tablespoons olive oil
small sliced onion
1 tablespoon chopped parsley
salt and freshly ground black pepper
flour
oil for deep frying
sprigs of parsley
tomato sauce (p. 179)

Wipe the fillets, put in a shallow dish, sprinkle with lemon juice, oil, onion, parsley, salt, and freshly ground black pepper, and leave to stand for 45–50 minutes, turning from time to time.

Drain the fillets, roll in flour, deep fry for 5 minutes, drain, arrange on a napkin-covered dish, garnish with sprigs of fresh or fried parsley, and serve. Serve tomato sauce separately.

Sole Veronique

Put the fish in an oven-proof dish, cover with milk, and poach in the oven at 350 °F (180 °C). Toss the mushrooms in 1½ tablespoons butter, season. Drain fillets (keeping the liquid) and put them in a buttered oven-proof dish. Cook flour in the rest of the butter, dilute with the milk left from poaching the fillets to make white sauce, stir until it thickens, add cheese and cream, and blend well. Put the mushrooms and grapes around the fillets, cover with sauce, bake in a hot oven at 450 °F (230 °C) for 10 minutes, and serve.

4 Servings
4 fillets of sole
1 pint (½ litre) milk
4 oz (100 g) sliced mushrooms
4 tablespoons butter
seasoning
2 tablespoons flour
3 tablespoons grated cheese
¼ pint (100 ml) cream
6 oz (150 g) peeled white grapes

Grilled Mackerel with Gooseberry Sauce

Fillet the mackerel, wash, dry, and dip in flour seasoned with a pinch of salt and a grating of pepper. Brush with melted butter and grill, basting with butter from time to time and allowing 4 minutes for each side. Top and tail the gooseberries, add sugar, and stew with a little water. Put through a blender. Add nutmeg, stir, boil down if the sauce needs thickening, and serve with mackerel.

4 Servings
4 mackerel about 10 oz (250 g) each
2 tablespoons seasoned flour
1 oz (25 g) butter
½ lb (200 g) gooseberries
½ teaspoon sugar (optional)
¼ teaspoon grated nutmeg

Swedish Mackerel Casserole

Put the fillets in a buttered casserole, skin side down. Season with salt, cover with leeks, tomatoes, and dill. Sprinkle with paprika and lemon juice and pour sour cream over the top. Cover and bake in hot oven at 425 °F (220 °C) for 30 minutes.

4 Servings
4 filleted mackerel
butter
salt
2 finely shredded leeks
½ lb (200 g) peeled, chopped tomatoes
1 tablespoon chopped dill (or parsley)
¼ teaspoon paprika
juice of ½ lemon
4 oz (100 g) sour cream

Sardine Meringue, Portuguese Style

Drain the sardines, remove tails and bones, mash, and mix with white sauce. Season to taste, if the sauce is hot, allow to cool. Add egg yolks, stir well and pour into a lightly buttered soufflé dish. Beat the egg whites with a small pinch of salt until stiff, pile over the sardine mixture. Smooth the top lightly and decorate by carefully arranging a layer of thin onion rings in whatever pattern pleases you. Put an olive, stuffing upwards, in the centre of each onion ring, put in the oven pre-heated to 375 °F (190 °C), bake for 25–30 minutes, and serve.

4 Servings
1 large tin sardines
½ pint (250 ml) white sauce (p. 178)
seasoning
3 egg yolks
butter
3 egg whites
onions cut in rings
stuffed olives

Soups

French Mussel Soup

4 Servings
2 quarts (2 litres) mussels
4 oz (100 ml) dry white wine
2 teaspoons chopped parsley
salt
small bouquet garni
butter
2 finely chopped onions
1 crushed clove garlic
1 pint (½ litre) boiling water
4 oz (100 ml) scalded milk
pepper
8 slices French bread
2 raw egg yolks
4 oz (100 ml) cream
juice of 1 lemon

Scrape and wash mussels thoroughly. Put in a pan with white wine, parsley, ½ teaspoon salt, and bouquet garni. Boil for 4–5 minutes until the mussels open. Keep warm. Strain the pan juices through double muslin and keep. In a large saucepan heat 2 oz (50 g) butter and gently fry onions and garlic until pale golden. Add strained mussel liquor, boiling water, and milk. Bring to the boil, then simmer for 15 minutes. Taste, add salt if necessary, and season with pepper.

Take mussels out of their shells and add to soup.

Fry slices of bread in butter and keep hot.

Beat egg yolks and cream in a soup tureen, stir in lemon juice, pour hot soup over the mixture. Serve with fried bread.

Beef Tea

3 lb (1½ kg) lean beef (shin or round)
2 pints (1 litre) cold water
salt

Wash and dry the meat, remove all fat and skin. Scrape, mince or chop the meat finely. Add water, stir, cover, and leave to stand for 20–30 minutes. Put to cook in a double saucepan, cover, simmer for 2½–3 hours, stirring from time to time. Strain, season, chill, and skim off any fat.

To serve, heat in a cup placed in hot water, adding more salt if necessary.

Pot-au-Feu

8 Servings
4 lb (2 kg) beef with bones (round, chuck or rib)
5 quarts (5 litres) cold water
1 tablespoon salt
1 bunch carrots
12 oz (300 g) turnips
6 young leeks
1 stalk celery
1 medium-sized onion
1 clove garlic
2 cloves
1 sprig thyme
½ bay leaf

Put the meat, tied with string, and the bones into a large pot. Add water and salt. Bring to the boil slowly, skimming off the scum which rises to the surface. Repeat this skimming operation two or three times, adding a few tablespoons of cold water each time to slow down the boiling process. Add the vegetables and other ingredients, bring to the boil once more, cover with a lid, and simmer gently for at least 4 hours.

If young vegetables are used, add them to the stock-pot after the meat has been cooking for 2 hours. Slow cooking is the secret of the pot-au-feu's clean, savoury taste and good amber colour.

To serve, skim off surplus fat, taste for seasoning, add more salt if necessary, and strain the broth into a soup tureen.

Serve the meat and vegetables separately with a sauce, grated horseradish or mustard.

Scotch Broth

Soak barley in enough cold water to cover overnight. Put the lamb in a pan with water, bring to the boil and remove scum.

Peel the onions, wash the peel and add to pan, together with bouquet garni. Peel adds to the richness of colour. Simmer 1½ hours.

Chop the onion finely and fry lightly in butter, without allowing it to brown. Extract bouquet garni and onion peel from the pan. Put in onions, carrot, turnip, and celery. Simmer for 30 minutes.

Take the meat out of the broth. Remove and discard all bones. Shred the meat and put back into pan. Drain barley and add to broth. Season to taste, simmer for 1 hour. Just before serving, sprinkle with chopped parsley.

6 Servings
3 oz (75 g) pearl barley
1 scrag end of lamb, roughly chopped
2¼ quarts (2¼ litres) water
2 onions
bouquet garni
1 tablespoon butter
4 oz (100 g) diced carrot
4 oz (100 g) diced turnip
3–4 shredded stalks celery
salt and pepper
1 tablespoon chopped parsley

French Oxtail Soup

Chop the oxtail into joints, roll in flour, and brown in hot oil. Add onion, carrot, celery, water, bay leaf, and barley. Bring to the boil, simmer for 2 hours. Season with salt and pepper and continue to simmer for another hour. Take the tail pieces out, bone, and put the meat back in the soup. Add wine, simmer for 5 minutes, sprinkle with parsley, and serve.

6 Servings
1¼ lb (750 g) oxtail
flour
2–3 tablespoons oil
1 chopped onion
1 chopped carrot
8 oz (200 g) shredded celery
3 pints (1¼ litres) water
1 bay leaf
1 tablespoon washed pearl barley
1 teaspoon salt
¼ teaspoon pepper
4 oz (100 ml) red wine
2 tablespoons chopped parsley

Beef Dishes

Parsleyed Beef

Put the beef in a pan with stock and parsley. Simmer for 10 minutes. Add lemon juice and simmer for another 10 minutes. Season to taste and serve piping hot with plain boiled rice.

4 Servings
8–12 slices boiled beef
½ pint (250 ml) hot stock
3–4 tablespoons chopped parsley
juice of 1 lemon
salt and freshly ground black pepper

Carbonnade à la Flamande

Cut the beef into 1 in. (2 cm) cubes. Fry onion in butter or margarine, add meat, and brown. Add sugar, French mustard, thyme and bay leaf, season, sprinkle with flour, and cover with pale ale. Bring to the boil, and stir. Cover and simmer for 2 hours.

4 Servings
2 lb (1 kg) lean stewing steak
1 sliced onion
2 oz (50 g) butter or margarine
1 lump sugar
1 teaspoon French mustard
sprig thyme
½ bay leaf
salt and black pepper
1 tablespoon flour
½ pint (250 ml) pale ale

Beef Stroganoff

6 Servings
1½ lb (750 g) fillet of beef
2 tablespoons flour
1 teaspoon salt
½ teaspoon dry mustard
½ teaspoon pepper
2 medium-sized onions
4 oz (100 g) butter
4 oz (100 g) sliced mushrooms
1 tablespoon brandy
1 tablespoon tomato purée
½ pint (250 ml) stock
1–2 tablespoons lemon juice
4 oz (100 ml) sour cream
1 tablespoon chopped parsley

Wash the meat, dry, trim away gristle, and cut into strips about 1 in. (2–3 cm) long and not more than ¼ in. (½ cm) thick. Mix flour with salt, mustard, and pepper. Slice the onions and fry in butter. Add mushrooms, fry together for 2–3 minutes, remove from heat. Dip meat strips in seasoned flour and shake off surplus. Brown the meat in hot butter, add onions and mushrooms with their pan juices. Fry together on low heat for 5 minutes, stirring with a wooden fork.

Sprinkle in the brandy, set it alight, then put in tomato purée, dilute with stock, and bring to the boil. Add lemon juice and sour cream, stir, cover with a lid, and simmer gently for 15 minutes. Bring to the boil, sprinkle with chopped parsley, and serve with new potatoes.

Steak Diane

4 Servings
4 thin fillet steaks
2 oz (50 g) butter
salt and freshly ground pepper
1 medium-sized chopped onion
1–2 crushed cloves garlic
1½ teaspoons French mustard
1 teaspoon Worcester sauce
2 tablespoons brandy
3 tablespoons cream or red wine

Beat the steaks gently to flatten and make very thin. Quickly cook on both sides in butter, season with salt and pepper, remove, and keep warm. In the same fat, fry onion and garlic. Add mustard and blend in well. Stir in Worcester sauce. Put steaks into pan, flame with brandy. As soon as the flames subside, add cream or wine, heat to bubbling point, and serve.

Biftecks au Roquefort

4 Servings
4 steaks
2 tablespoons butter
2 oz (50 g) Roquefort cheese
salt and freshly grated black pepper

Grill the steaks, about 2–3 minutes each side. Blend butter with Roquefort. Arrange steaks on a heated serving dish, season to taste, put a dollop of Roquefort mixture on each, and serve at once.

Steak au Poivre

6 Servings
6 steaks
1½ teaspoons peppercorns
2 tablespoons butter
2 tablespoons oil
4 oz (100 ml) stock
1½ tablespoons brandy (optional)
pinch cornstarch
salt

Trim the steaks. Crush the peppercorns in a cloth. Do not grind them as this would make the pepper too fine. Coat both sides of the steaks with crushed peppercorns, pressing well to make them adhere. Fry in mixture of butter and oil, remove, and keep warm. Dilute the pan juices with stock, add brandy, sprinkle in cornstarch, simmer, stirring until the sauce glazes, check seasoning, pour over the steaks, and serve.

Bœuf Bourguignon

2 lb (1 kg) lean beef
½ pint (250 ml) red wine

Marinate the beef in red wine with the parsley, thyme,

and bay leaf, for 3 hours. Remove the beef and strain the marinade. Melt dripping in a pan, fry onion till golden, add beef, brown it. Remove, stir in flour, add stock – slowly stirring as you do so – then add the wine in which the beef was marinated. Replace the beef in this sauce and simmer, covered for 3 hours. Slice the mushrooms and fry them in 1 oz (25 g) dripping with button onions until golden. Season to taste. Place the beef on a hot dish, surround it with mushrooms and onions, and serve the sauce in which the beef has cooked in a sauce-boat.

⅓ pint (200 ml) red wine
4 sprigs parsley
sprig thyme
1 bay leaf
3 oz (75 g) dripping
1 sliced onion
1 tablespoon flour
4 oz (100 ml) meat stock
4 oz (100 g) button mushrooms
12 button onions
salt and pepper

Fondue Bourguignonne

8 Servings
2 lb (1 kg) good steak
1 pint (½ litre) oil
mayonnaise (p. 57)
tomato sauce (p. 179)
horseradish sauce (p. 179)

This French dish has been invented to relieve the hostess of doing the cooking; the guests cook their own meal! All you need do is to provide the raw ingredients and the sauces, a cooking pan standing over a spirit lamp or other source of heat in the middle of the table, and a long-handled fork for each guest. Each guest cooks a cube of meat on his fork, then dips it into one of the sauces, both to flavour and cool the meat.

Make your sauces and arrange them in bowls on the table around the cooking pan. Cut meat into bite-size cubes. Heat oil in the pan, put it on the table burner, and your guests do the rest. Serve with crisp French bread.

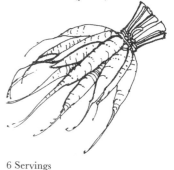

Bœuf à la Mode

6 Servings
lardoons of salt pork
2 lb (1 kg) rump steak
pinch thyme
¼ teaspoon origan
1 pint (½ litre) dry white wine
5 tablespoons butter
2 tablespoons brandy
1 calf's foot
piece of pork skin
3 sliced onions
4 medium-sized sliced carrots
2–3 sprigs parsley
a handful of celery leaves
10 crushed peppercorns
bouquet garni
4 oz (100 ml) water
salt and pepper

Cut the salt pork (or bacon fat) into strips and, with the aid of a larding needle, insert these into the beef. Put the beef in a dish, sprinkle with thyme and origan, cover with wine, and leave to marinate for a few hours. Drain, brown on all sides in half the butter, remove, put in a casserole, pour the brandy over the beef, and set it alight for a moment.

Add calf's foot and pork skin. Fry the onions, carrots, parsley, and celery leaves in the butter left from searing the beef, and add to the meat, together with pepper-corns, bouquet garni, the wine in which the beef was marinated, with all the spices and the water. Bring to the boil, cover, and simmer gently on top of the stove, or in the oven at 300 °F (150 °C) for 4 to 5 hours. Before serving, remove bouquet garni and pork skin, season to taste, and blend into the sauce the remainder of the butter, adding it in small pieces. Put the meat and the calf's foot on a serving dish, garnish with carrots and onions, strain the sauce over the meat, and serve with boiled or steamed potatoes.

Steak and Kidney Pudding

4 Servings
8 oz (200 g) self-raising flour
pinch salt
4 oz (100 g) finely shredded suet
cold water

Sift flour and salt into a mixing bowl, add suet, and mix well, moistening with a little cold water (about 6 tablespoons in all) and stirring with the blade of a knife until the paste is firm, pliable, and smooth. Roll out and use at once.

1 lb (½ kg) stewing steak
¼ lb (100 g) ox kidney
¼ lb (100 g) mushrooms
1 oz (25 g) flour
salt and pepper
1–2 tablespoons beef dripping
1 small chopped onion (optional)
pinch mixed chopped herbs
stock or water

On a lightly floured board, roll out the pastry thinly; it should not be more than ¼ in. (½ cm) thick. Using a 1½ pint (¾ litre) basin as a measure, cut a circle to be used as a lid. Collect the rest of the paste, roll out as before, and line a well-greased pudding basin with it. Cut the steak and kidney into bite-size pieces, removing all gristle and fat. Slice the mushrooms. Season the flour with salt and pepper, and roll the steak and kidney cubes in it. Heat the dripping, fry the onion in it until it becomes soft and transparent, add steak and kidney, sauté for 3 minutes to seal in the juices, and put into the pastry-lined basin in layers, scattering each layer with mushrooms and sprinkling with a minute pinch of mixed herbs. Add enough stock or water to fill the basin nearly to the top. Moisten the pastry edges, which should be neatly trimmed off, put on the pastry lid, press well to seal, and cover with a sheet of greaseproof paper or kitchen foil. Rinse out a clean linen cloth in boiling water, wring out, flour it, make a 1 in. (2 cm) pleat in the middle to allow for rising, and lay it over the pudding. Tie the cloth around the basin with string. and secure the four corners into two knots on top. Put the basin in a pan of boiling water (or steam in a steamer) and boil fast for 2 hours, filling up with boiling water as it evaporates. Reduce heat, and continue to cook for another 2 hours, replenishing the pan with boiling water to keep the level constantly about half-way up the pudding basin. Never attempt to hasten the cooking of a suet pudding; it really does need 3½–4 hours and is one of those rewarding and delicious dishes which almost cannot be overcooked.

When done, lift the pudding from the steamer or pan of boiling water, take off the cloth and greaseproof paper, tie a napkin around the basin and serve with a sauce-boat of good hot stock. When the pudding is cut, put in some stock to augment the gravy.

Bavarian Casserole

Keep the meat in one piece. Line a casserole with bacon rashers and cover with onions. Place the meat on this foundation, sprinkle with lemon juice and sugar, season to taste with salt, pepper, and nutmeg, add cloves and bay leaf, moisten with beer and equal amount of water, cover, and simmer slowly for 3 hours.

8 Servings
2 lb (1 kg) rump of beef
8 bacon rashers
2 sliced medium-sized onions
juice of 1 lemon
1 tablespoon brown sugar
salt and pepper
pinch nutmeg
2 cloves
½ bay leaf
1 pint (½ litre) beer
water

Irish Spiced Beef

Wash and dry the piece of meat. A week before this dish is to be eaten, grind the cloves, bay leaves, peppercorns, allspice, saltpetre, garlic, and sea salt in a mortar or grinder and mix well. Rub this powder all over the piece of meat. Put in an earthenware dish in a cool place. Each day for the rest of the week, rub the meat all over with the spiced juice from the dish.

On the day: rinse the meat under the cold tap and tie up if necessary. Place in a saucepan. Peel and slice the carrots and onions and arrange round the meat. Add bouquet garni. Barely cover with water, cover, and simmer for 4 hours. Add Guinness and simmer for another hour. Can be eaten hot, but is best cold with carrots from the pan and boiled potatoes.

4 Servings
1 lb (½ kg) beef
1 tablespoon cloves
3 bay leaves
1 tablespoon black peppercorns
1 teaspoon allspice
2 scant teaspoons saltpetre
1 clove garlic
1 lb (½ kg) sea salt
3 carrots
3 onions
1 bouquet garni
water
1 bottle Guinness

Oiseaux Sans Têtes – 'Headless Birds'

Cut the beef into thin slices, beat to flatten, put a piece of bacon and a small sprig of parsley on each, season to taste, roll up, and secure with thread. Dip in flour, fry in sizzling butter until brown all round, moisten with stock, add wine, cover, and simmer gently for 2 hours.

Discard threads before serving.

6 Servings
2 lb (1 kg) beef
8 oz (200 g) sliced bacon
parsley
salt and pepper
flour
butter
½ pint (250 ml) stock
4 oz (100 ml) dry red wine

Meat Balls in Sweet and Sour Tomato Sauce

Fry garlic and chopped onion in tablespoon oil, mix with minced beef, season to taste with salt and pepper. Add eggs and blend well.

Form into walnut-sized balls and fry in hot oil until uniformly brown. Transfer meat balls to a casserole. In the oil left from cooking the meat balls, fry sliced onions until soft, stir in flour, and cook together for 2–3 minutes. Add tomato purée and cook, stirring for 1 minute, little by little blend in stock. Check seasoning, add bay leaf, sugar, and lemon juice. Bring

6–8 Servings
1–2 pounded cloves garlic
1 finely chopped onion
5 tablespoons oil for frying
2 lb (1 kg) minced beef
salt and pepper
2 beaten eggs
2 thinly sliced onions
1 tablespoon flour
2 tablespoons tomato purée
½ pint (250 ml) stock
1 small bay leaf
1–1½ teaspoons sugar

juice of ⅓ lemon
1 tablespoon chopped dill or parsley

to the boil, then pour the sauce over the meat balls and put in a slow oven at 300 °F (150 °C) for 35–40 minutes. Sprinkle with chopped dill and serve with plain boiled rice.

Beef and Bacon Loaf

6 Servings
1 lb (½ kg) lean beef
1 lb (½ kg) bacon
1 medium-sized onion
8 oz (200 g) grated breadcrumbs
salt and pepper
pinch nutmeg
2 eggs
2–3 tablespoons butter or margarine

Mince beef, bacon, and onion. Add half the breadcrumbs, season with salt, pepper, and nutmeg to taste. Add eggs and mix well.

Put in a cloth, shape into loaf, tie the cloth securely and boil in water for 2½–3 hours. Drain and leave to cool. Unwrap, slice, arrange on a serving dish.

Fry remaining breadcrumbs in butter, sprinkle over loaf and serve.

Lamb and Mutton Dishes

Lamb Chops in Breadcrumbs, Italian Style

4 Servings
4 fairly thick loin chops
juice of 1 lemon
2 tablespoons oil
pinch each of thyme, rosemary, and
 origan
soft breadcrumbs
salt and pepper

Put the chops in a dish, sprinkle with lemon juice, half the oil, and herbs. Leave for 45–50 minutes. Drain chops, dry on kitchen paper, brush with remaining oil, dip in breadcrumbs, and season. Grill on very high heat. Serve with fresh garden peas.

Devonshire Chop Pie

4 Servings
1 tablespoon butter
2 large cooking apples, peeled, cored,
 and sliced
8 lamb or mutton chops
salt and pepper
2 sliced onions
½ pint (250 ml) stock or water
short crust pastry (p. 57)

Line the bottom of a lightly buttered pie dish with apple slices. Season chops to taste and put half of them on the apples and cover with a layer of sliced onion. Repeat this, finishing with a layer of onions. Spoon stock or water over the contents of the pie dish. Roll out pastry, cover pie with it, and put in the oven pre-heated to 450 °F (230 °C) for 10–15 minutes. Lower oven heat to 375 °F (190 °C) and continue to bake for 45–50 minutes.

Lamb, Swedish Style

7–8 Servings
4 lb (2 kg) leg of lamb
2 teaspoons salt
¼ teaspoon pepper
½ pint (250 ml) made coffee
1 teaspoon sugar
1 tablespoon cream
½ pint (250 ml) milk
1 tablespoon flour
1 teaspoon redcurrant jelly

Season lamb with salt and pepper, and roast in the oven at 375 °F (190 °C) for ½ hour. Mix coffee with sugar and cream and pour over roast. Continue to roast for 1 hour, basting from time to time. Strain liquid from pan and skim off fat. Add milk to pan juices. Using 2 tablespoons of skimmed-off fat and the flour make a roux, cook for several minutes, dilute with pan gravy mixed with milk, simmer, stirring until sauce thickens, check seasoning, and add redcurrant jelly. Arrange joint on a dish, serve sauce separately.

Creole Lamb Cutlets (Louisiana French recipe)

6 Servings
6 lamb chops
2 oz (50 g) butter
8 oz (200 g) rice
salt and pepper
4 oz (100 ml) water
4 oz (100 ml) milk
3 oz (75 g) sultanas
3 peeled and sliced bananas

Wash and dry the chops.

Melt half the butter in a frying pan, add rice, and stir until the rice has absorbed all the butter. Do not allow the rice to brown, so keep heat very low. Season to taste. Pour water and milk over the rice, add sultanas, cover and cook for about 20 minutes.

Brown the bananas in the remaining butter and keep warm. Grill the lamb chops. To be authentically Louisiana French, they should be underdone.

To serve, arrange the chops on rice and decorate with fried bananas.

Minted Lamb Chops

4 Servings
4 thickly cut lamb chops
4 oz (100 ml) oil
4 tablespoons lemon juice
4 oz (100 g) mint jelly
salt and pepper

Have the chops cut about 2 in. (5 cm) thick. Put in a dish, sprinkle with oil and lemon juice, and leave for 1–2 hours.

Heat the grill. Take chops out of marinade and grill under medium heat, turning after 12–13 minutes to brown the other side. Do not overcook.

Melt mint jelly over simmering water and use for basting chops during grilling. Just before serving, season to taste.

Lemon Lamb

4 Servings
1¼ lb (750 g) stewing lamb
3 tablespoons oil
1 thinly sliced lemon
¼ teaspoon cinnamon
salt and pepper
small pinch saffron
¼ pint (250 ml) hot stock

Cut the lamb into uniform pieces, and brown in oil. Cover with lemon slices, sprinkle with cinnamon, and season to taste with salt and freshly ground pepper. Dilute saffron in hot stock, add to pan, stir well, cover and simmer gently for 1 hour, or until the lamb is tender.

Old English Boiled Mutton with Caper Sauce

8–10 Servings
one 5 lb (2¼ kg) leg of mutton
water
salt
1 small sliced onion
1 sliced carrot
1 small stalk celery
caper sauce (p. 179)

Wash and dry the meat. Bring unsalted water to the boil and put in meat. Make sure the whole leg is submerged in the water. Allow the water to come to the boil again, then reduce heat and simmer for 1 hour, skimming off all the scum which rises to the surface. Add the rest of the ingredients, except the sauce, of course, and continue to simmer for another 1½–2 hours.

Drain the meat and put on a hot serving dish or a

carving board. Keep the liquor in which it was cooked as stock, to be strained and degreased for future use.

Serve with boiled carrots and mashed turnips with butter. Pass caper sauce separately.

Lamb with Chestnuts

4 Servings
3 tablespoons butter
2 lb (1 kg) neck of lamb
1 large chopped onion
2 large thinly sliced carrots
salt and pepper
2 tablespoons chopped parsley
4 oz (100 ml) dry white wine
1 lb (½ kg) chestnuts

Heat the butter in a pan large enough eventually to take all ingredients. Brown the piece of lamb evenly all around. Add onions and carrots, sauté until the vegetables are coated with a film of fat and begin to look glazed. Season, sprinkle with parsley, moisten with wine, cover, and simmer gently for 2 hours.

Slit the chestnuts on the pointed side, put them in a tin with a little water, roast in the oven for 10 minutes, and peel while hot. Add to the casserole, cook for a further half hour and serve.

Lamb Vindaloo

4 Servings
1 lb (½ kg) lamb
4 tablespoons butter
2–3 chopped cloves garlic
2 medium-sized chopped onions
2 tablespoons vindaloo paste (p. 180)
2 tablespoons lime (or lemon) juice
salt

Cut the lamb into bite-size pieces. Heat the butter and gently fry garlic and onions until soft. Add vindaloo paste and lime juice. Stir and simmer very gently for 5 minutes, taking care not to burn the mixture. Add lamb to pan, mix well, moisten with 4 oz (100 ml) water, cover, and simmer until tender. Serve with rice.

Veal Dishes

Veal Chops with Tarragon

4 Servings
4 veal chops
flour
3 tablespoons oil
4 oz (100 ml) dry white wine
2 tablespoons tomato paste
16–20 chopped fresh tarragon leaves
salt and pepper
paprika

Dredge chops with flour and fry in hot oil to brown on both sides. Cover, reduce heat, and simmer for 20 minutes, turning from time to time. Add wine, stir it well in to incorporate all the juices. Blend in tomato paste, and two-thirds of the tarragon, season with salt and pepper. Cook for 10 minutes. Transfer chops to a heated dish, pour sauce over them, sprinkle with remaining chopped tarragon and paprika, and serve.

Osso Buco

6 Servings
2¼–3 lb (1–1¼ kg) shin bone veal
flour
salt and pepper
6 tablespoons oil
1 chopped onion
2 small diced carrots
½ bay leaf

Have the veal sawn into 2 in. (5 cm) pieces, wipe with a damp cloth. Season flour with salt and pepper and roll the chunks of shin in it, then brown in oil for 10 minutes. Remove from frying pan, and fit the bones in a sauté pan in an upright position to prevent the bone marrow flowing out. In the fat left from browning the bones, fry the onion, carrots, bay leaf, and celery for a few minutes, to soften the vegetables and to give them a film coating of oil. Moisten with wine, cook to reduce the wine by half, and add the mixture to the bones.

Add stock and tomatoes, cover and simmer for 2 hours. (Do not allow the sauce to dry out. Add more stock and wine, if necessary.) Carefully remove the veal on to a serving dish and keep warm. Strain the sauce, put back in a pan, reheat, and pour over the veal. Mix parsley, garlic, and lemon peel, sprinkle over osso buco and serve with plain rice.

1–2 stalks diced celery
¼ pint (100 ml) dry white wine
¼ pint (100 ml) veal stock
2 lb (1 kg) ripe, peeled, diced tomatoes
2 tablespoons chopped parsley
1 clove chopped garlic
1 tablespoon grated lemon peel

Veal Chops with Orange Sauce

Trim and flatten the chops slightly, brown in butter until golden, then simmer gently until done. Grill or fry the bacon and keep warm. Cut the peel off one orange very thinly, without any pith, shred, parboil for a few minutes, and drain.

Season the chops to taste, arrange on a dish, garnish with bacon rashers, and keep warm.

Blend the flour into the fat left in the pan, dilute with orange juice, add orange peel, simmer for 2–3 minutes, season, and remove from heat. Whisk the egg with cream, add to the sauce, pour over the chops, and serve.

6 Servings
6 veal chops
4 tablespoons butter
6 bacon rashers
peel of 1 and juice of 2 oranges
salt and pepper
½ tablespoon flour
1 egg
6 tablespoons double cream

Veal Escalopes Flamed in Brandy with Asparagus Tips

Fry the escalopes in butter, brown both sides, add asparagus, and simmer until both are tender. Sprinkle with brandy, set aflame, baste the escalopes with the blazing brandy, blend in cream, stir, season to taste, simmer for 2 minutes, and serve.

4 Servings
4 veal escalopes
3 tablespoons butter
1 lb (½ kg) asparagus, trimmed and parboiled
2 tablespoons brandy
6 tablespoons cream
salt and pepper

Veal with Green Peppers

Cut the veal into bite-size cubes. Wash and slice the peppers. Brown veal in butter, season to taste. Add tomatoes, cover, and simmer for 20 minutes. Heat oil, fry onions until soft, add peppers. Cook gently until tender, add to veal, stir, taste for seasoning. Add wine, cover, simmer for 20 minutes, and serve.

6 Servings
1½ lb (750 g) lean veal
4 seeded green peppers
3 oz (75 g) butter
salt and pepper
8 oz (200 g) peeled tomatoes
3 tablespoons oil
2 medium-sized sliced onions
4 oz (100 ml) dry white wine

6 Servings
2lb (1 kg) veal
butter
2 tablespoons olive oil
2 medium-sized sliced onions
1 sliced carrot
2 cloves garlic, crushed
salt
freshly ground pepper
2 tablespoons flour
4 oz (100 ml) dry white wine
1 lb (½ kg) peeled, chopped tomatoes
bouquet garni
1 pint (½ litre) veal stock
1 dozen small onions
8 oz (200 g) mushrooms
juice of ¼ lemon
1 tablespoon chopped parsley
croûtons (p. 181)

Veal Marengo

Cut veal into large cubes. Heat 4 tablespoons butter and the oil in a sauté pan and sauté veal for 5 minutes with the onions, carrot, and garlic. Season with salt and freshly ground pepper, sprinkle with flour, allow to colour slightly. Add wine, reduce by two-thirds, and add tomatoes. Put in bouquet garni and enough stock to cover the meat. Bring to the boil, cover and simmer gently for 1 hour.

Scald the little onions, drain, dry with a cloth, and cook in 1 tablespoon butter until golden.

Clean and drain mushrooms (if large, cut into quarters). In a large casserole, heat 2 tablespoons butter. Lightly fry the mushrooms and remove from heat.

When the veal is almost tender, remove with a perforated spoon, and lay on top of the mushrooms. Cover with onions. Allow the sauce to stand for a few minutes, skim, and strain over the veal, pressing garnish through with a wooden spoon. Check seasoning and simmer until veal is completely cooked, about 15–20 minutes.

Sprinkle with lemon juice and chopped parsley and garnish with croûtons fried in butter.

4 Servings
2 lb (1 kg) veal
1 onion
2 oz (50 ml) olive oil
1–2 crushed cloves garlic
12 oz (300 g) peeled fresh or tinned
   tomatoes
pinch rosemary
salt and freshly ground black pepper
4 tablespoons port

Veal à la Provençale

Cut the meat into uniform bite-sized pieces. Slice onion and fry in oil until soft. Add garlic and cook for 2 minutes. Put in meat and brown all over. Add the rest of the ingredients, season to taste. Cover, reduce heat, and simmer gently until tender, stirring from time to time. Serve with plain boiled rice or macaroni.

4 Servings
4 veal escalopes
flour
salt and pepper
butter
8 oz (200 g) mushrooms
1 tablespoon chopped onions
3 eggs
1 tablespoon chopped parsley
4 sliced tomatoes
2 oz (50 g) grated cheese

Veal Escalopes with Egg and Mushroom Topping

Beat escalopes to make them thin. Coat with flour seasoned with salt and pepper. Heat enough butter to brown the escalopes and seal the juices. Reduce heat and continue to cook the escalopes for another couple of minutes on each side. Remove, drain, and put in a fireproof dish. Slice mushrooms and fry lightly with onion.

Beat eggs, season with salt and pepper, mix with parsley, and scramble until just set.

Spoon the egg mixture neatly on top of escalopes, cover with slices of tomato, sprinkle with cheese, and brown the surface quickly under the grill.

Italian Veal Croquettes

Chop the mushrooms and lightly fry in butter. Add meat, season with salt and pepper. Moisten with Madeira, stir, cover and simmer over very low heat for 5 minutes. Mix with Béchamel, check seasoning, and allow to cool. Shape into uniform croquettes, roll first in flour, then in breadcrumbs, and deep fry until golden. Drain well, arrange on a dish, garnish with fried parsley, and serve with tomato or mushroom sauce.

4 Servings
4 oz (100 g) mushrooms
2–3 tablespoons butter
1 lb (½ kg) minced cooked veal
salt and pepper
4 tablespoons Madeira
½ pint (250 ml) thick Béchamel
   Sauce (p. 143)
flour
breadcrumbs
fat for deep frying
fried parsley (p. 181)

Veal and Ham Pie

Have the pastry ready for final rolling out. Cut veal into 1½ in. (4 cm) squares and the ham into strips. Heat butter and gently sauté the veal without letting it colour at all. Arrange the veal, ham, and eggs in a pie dish in layers, seasoning each layer and sprinkling it with mixed herbs, nutmeg, onion, parsley, and lemon rind. Pour in enough stock to fill the dish three parts full.

Roll out the pastry, cover the pie dish with it, make a hole in the top, and slip in a paper 'chimney' to allow steam to escape. Brush with beaten egg mixed with a tiny pinch of salt. Bake in a moderately hot oven at 400 °F (200 °C) for about half an hour.

Serve hot or cold.

6 Servings
8 oz (200 g) flaky pastry (p. 186)
1½ lb (750 g) fillet of veal
¾ lb (300 g) ham
2 tablespoons butter
3 quartered hard-boiled eggs
salt and pepper
pinch mixed herbs
pinch nutmeg
1 tablespoon finely chopped onion
1 tablespoon finely chopped parsley
¼ teaspoon grated lemon rind
½ pint (250 ml) jellied veal stock
1 beaten egg

Pork Dishes

Roast Pork à la Boulangère

If the joint is boned, ask the butcher to tie it. Butter an oven dish, line it with apples, then cover with sliced potatoes. Put the pork on potatoes, season, sprinkle with rosemary, and roast in the oven pre-heated to 400 °F (200 °C) for about an hour, or until the meat is nicely browned. Cover with buttered foil and continue to roast until done. Serve in the same dish.

6 Servings
3 lb (1½ kg) pork loin
3 tablespoons butter
3 peeled, cored, and sliced apples
6 peeled sliced potatoes
salt and pepper
teaspoon rosemary

Pork Chops, Swiss Style

Trim the chops and fry in butter until brown on both sides. Season with salt and freshly ground black pepper, keep warm. Mix cheese with cream and mustard to taste, then coat the chops with the mixture on one side. Put under a hot grill to brown the surface and serve.

2 Servings
2 pork chops
1 tablespoon butter
salt and pepper
2 oz (50 g) grated Gruyère cheese
3 tablespoons double cream
French mustard

4 lb (2 kg) cut of back bacon
1 quart (1 litre) water
1 onion
2–3 cloves
sprig parsley
sprig thyme
pinch rosemary
1 sliced carrot
10–12 peppercorns
2 tablespoons Demerara sugar
apple sauce (p. 73)

Boiled Bacon

Soak bacon overnight, rinse, drain, put in a pan with water, onion, cloves, parsley, thyme, rosemary, carrot, and peppercorns. Bring to the boil, skim, cover, and simmer for 1½ hours. Allow to cool in the cooking liquid.

Drain bacon, skin, rub with Demerara sugar, put in a pan, moisten with 1 to 2 tablespoons of the cooking liquor, and put in a hot oven 425 °F (220 °C) for 10–15 minutes to glaze the surface. Serve with apple sauce.

Braised Ham

Soak the ham in cold water for several hours, then put into a pan of cold unseasoned water, bring to the boil, and simmer on lowest possible heat (so that the surface of the water does no more than 'shiver'), allowing 20 minutes per pound (½ kg). Take it out of the poaching liquid 40 minutes before the end of cooking. Skin, put into a braising pan, which should be just big enough to contain the ham. Moisten with 1 pint (½ litre) of whatever wine you decide to use – Madeira, Marsala, Frontignan – cover, and cook in the oven for three-quarters of an hour. Before serving, drain, sprinkle with icing sugar, and brown in the oven or under a grill.

Poached Ham

Soak the ham in cold water for several hours, then put into a pan of cold unseasoned water and bring to the boil. Simmer on low heat, allowing 20 minutes per pound (½ kg). If the ham is to be served cold, leave it to cool in the cooking water.

To glaze a ham which is to be served hot, poach as above, skin, sprinkle with icing sugar, and brown in the oven or under a grill.

Ham, Grilled

If the ham is mild, do not soak it. If it needs soaking, do this some time before it is to be grilled and pat dry on a cloth.

Have the slice about ½ in. (1 cm) thick. Trim off the rind and cut through the fat to the meat at intervals of 1–2 in. (2–5 cm). Brush the lean part of the ham with a little bacon fat and place it under a hot grill. Grill one side and then the other at full, then reduce the heat and finish off both sides.

Hawaiian Ham with Bananas and Coconut

Pre-heat oven to 350 °F (180 °C).

Grease a baking dish with half a tablespoon butter. Put thick slices of ham in it, cover them with banana slices. Sprinkle with sugar, coconut, and lemon juice. Scatter remaining butter over the surface in tiny pieces and bake for 30 minutes.

4 Servings
1–2 tablespoons butter
4 thick slices of ham
2 peeled sliced bananas
4 tablespoons brown sugar
4 tablespoons coconut flakes
juice of ¼ lemon

Ham with Tarragon Sauce

Have the ham cut into slices about ¼ in. (½ cm) thick. Bring the wine to the boil and reduce by half. Add two sprigs tarragon and leave on lowest possible heat to infuse without boiling. Chop the third tarragon sprig. Heat half the butter, stir flour into it, and cook a smooth roux. Blend in stock, season, stir until smooth. Very gradually blend in tarragon-flavoured wine, keeping on very low heat so that the sauce remains fairly thin. Heat the remaining butter and heat the ham slices through, without actually frying them. Arrange them slightly overlapping, on a heated serving dish. Strain the sauce over them and serve with new potatoes.

4 Servings
8 slices of cooked ham
¼ pint (250 ml) dry white wine
3 sprigs tarragon
4 tablespoons butter
1 tablespoon flour
4 oz (100 ml) stock
salt and pepper

Offal Dishes

Brain Fritters

Soak brains for 15–20 minutes in cold water with a little vinegar added to it. Rinse under running cold water, removing all membranes and clots. Cover with fresh cold water and leave to soak for an hour, changing the water from time to time. Then to blanch the brains, drop into boiling court-bouillon or salted water. Reduce heat, simmer gently for 10 minutes, and drain thoroughly.

Mix flour with a pinch of salt and enough water to give batter the consistency of double cream. Just before using, fold in egg whites.

Pre-heat deep fat.

Cut brains into squares, dip in batter, and deep fry until golden brown. Drain, sprinkle with fine dry salt, garnish with fried parsley, and serve.

4 Servings
vinegar
2 sets calves brains
court-bouillon (p. 180)
4 oz (100 g) flour
salt
water
2 stiffly beaten egg whites
fat for deep frying
fried parsley (p. 181)

Fried Sweetbreads

4 Servings
2 pairs calves' sweetbreads
1 beaten egg
breadcrumbs
butter or margarine
slivers of truffle
cooked asparagus tips

Soak sweetbreads in water for 1 hour. Put in a sauce-pan, cover with cold salted water, bring to the boil, simmer for 5 minutes. Cool under running water, drain, and trim. Cut the sweetbreads into slices, dip in beaten egg and breadcrumbs, fry in butter or margarine. Garnish with slivers of truffle and cooked asparagus tips. Sprinkle with juices left in the pan.

Oxtail with Sausages

6 Servings
2 oxtails
4 tablespoons dripping or lard
1 pint (½ litre) stock
4 oz (100 ml) dry white wine
bouquet garni
salt and freshly ground black pepper
1 lb (½ kg) chipolata sausages

Cut the tails into chunks. Heat dripping, put in oxtail, add stock, cover and simmer for 15 minutes. Add the rest of ingredients, except sausages. Reduce heat to lowest possible and simmer very gently under a lid for 3½–4 hours. If after that time the gravy is not thick enough, uncover and reduce to concentrate it.

Put in sausages, simmer for 15 minutes, check seasoning, and serve.

Tongue with Olives, Italian Style

4 Servings
1 calf's tongue
water
salt
1 medium-sized onion
1 medium-sized carrot
1 oz (25 g) butter
½ pint (250 ml) veal stock
8 large chopped olives

Put the tongue in a pan, cover with cold water, bring to the boil. Skim, add a little salt, simmer for 1½ hours. Drain, allow to cool, and skin.

Dice the onion and carrot, and fry in butter. Add tongue, brown on all sides, add stock and olives, cover, simmer on very low heat for 1 hour, and serve.

Kidney, Belgian Style

2 Servings
2 calf's kidneys
2 tablespoons butter
salt and pepper
4 crushed juniper berries
2 tablespoons gin
1½ tablespoons thickened veal stock

Trim all fat off kidneys, remove membranes.

Heat the butter in a sauté pan, cook the kidneys. Season with salt and pepper. At the last moment add juniper berries and gin, set ablaze, and extinguish the flames with thickened veal stock. Serve.

Kidneys in Madeira

2–3 Servings
2 calf's kidneys
4 oz (100 g) sliced mushrooms
4 tablespoons olive oil
4 tablespoons Madeira
2 tablespoons chopped parsley
salt and pepper

Wash the kidneys, remove all fat and membranes, rinse in cold water, and slice. Rinse the mushrooms, without allowing them to soak in the water, dry on a cloth, and slice. Heat the oil, and sauté the kidneys on a high flame for 2 minutes, stirring frequently. Reduce heat, add mushrooms, Madeira, and half the parsley. Stir, season to taste, simmer gently for 10 minutes, remove from pan, transfer to a heated serving dish, and sprinkle with the rest of the parsley.

Liver, Italian Style

Heat a little oil, enough to cover the bottom of a heavy pan. Slice the onions very thinly and cook them very gently, keeping the heat very low, for half an hour. Cut the liver into very thin slices, lightly dredge with flour, and fry to brown both sides for 2 minutes. Season to taste. Spoon the liver on top of onions and serve at once.

4 Servings
olive oil
4 large onions
1 lb (½ kg) calf's liver
flour
salt and pepper

Calf's Liver Bercy

Cut the liver into thin slices, season with salt and pepper, dredge lightly with flour, brush with butter, and grill. Arrange on a dish and serve with Bercy butter.

4 Servings
1 lb (½ kg) calf's liver
salt and pepper
flour
1 tablespoon butter
Bercy butter (p. 178)

Liver Soufflé

Purée cooked liver in a blender with butter and Béchamel sauce. Bind with egg yolks and double cream, season with salt, pepper, and nutmeg. At the last moment fold in stiffly beaten egg whites. Pour into a buttered soufflé dish, filling it to about two-thirds. Cook in a pre-heated oven at 400 °F (200 °C) for 20–25 minutes. Serve immediately.

4 Servings
1 lb (½ kg) braised calf's or lambs liver
4 tablespoons butter
½ pint (250 ml) very thick Béchamel sauce (p. 143)
3 egg yolks
4 tablespoons double cream
salt and pepper
nutmeg
3 stiffly beaten egg whites

Chicken Dishes

Chicken Maryland

Wash and dry the chicken pieces. Season them, dip in flour, then in egg and breadcrumbs. Fry in ½ in. (1 cm) hot fat until uniformly brown. Reduce heat and cook until tender. Drain and keep warm in a moderate oven.

Cut the bananas in half lengthways, dip in egg and breadcrumbs, and fry for a few minutes. Arrange chicken portions on a serving dish, garnish with fried bananas, bacon rolls, and corn fritters, decorate with bunches of watercress and serve with cream gravy.

6 Servings
one 3 lb (1½ kg) roasting chicken cut in portions
salt and pepper
6 oz (150 g) flour
2 beaten eggs
6 oz (150 g) breadcrumbs
fat for frying
3 bananas
grilled bacon rolls (p 180)
corn fritters (p. 180)
watercress
cream gravy (p. 179)

Paprika Chicken with Dumplings, Hungarian Style

Start by preparing the batter for the dumplings. Mix flour with a tablespoon salt, the egg, and cold water until well blended. Leave to stand for 45–50 minutes.

Brown the chicken pieces on both sides in bacon dripping and butter over a high flame. Push to one

4–5 Servings
8 oz (200 g) flour
1 egg
6 fl. oz (150 ml) cold water
1 jointed chicken
2 tablespoons melted bacon fat
2 tablespoons butter
1 finely chopped onion

1 seeded, sliced green pepper
8 oz (200 ml) peeled, sliced tomatoes
salt and white pepper
1 tablespoon paprika
¼ pint (250 ml) hot stock or water
¼ pint (250 ml) sour cream
1 teaspoon kneaded butter (optional)

6 Servings
4 lb (2 kg) capon
3 tablespoons butter
3 oz (75 g) diced lean pork belly
*   or 6 slices lean bacon*
2 dozen baby onions
6–8 oz (150–200 g) quartered
*   mushrooms*
3 tablespoons heated brandy
1 bottle red Burgundy wine
chicken stock
salt and pepper
1–2 cloves crushed garlic
bouquet garni
1 tablespoon kneaded butter (p. 72)
chicken liver
croûtons

side of the skillet and add onion. As soon as the onion becomes transparent, add green pepper and tomatoes. Cook together for 3–4 minutes, season with salt and white pepper to taste, sprinkle with paprika, moisten with stock, bring to the boil, cover, turn down heat to low, and simmer for 35–40 minutes or until the chicken is tender. Turn the chicken joints from time to time to prevent sticking, moistening with a little more stock if necessary. When the chicken is tender, take it out of the pan and keep hot, preferably over steam.

Add sour cream to the pan juices, stir well, thicken if necessary with kneaded butter, incorporating it into the sauce in small pieces. Check seasoning.

When the chicken is nearly done, start cooking the dumplings. Boil them as you would pasta, in plenty of salted boiling water, dropping the batter into it a teaspoon at a time. Don't put in too many at once. As soon as the dumplings float up to the surface, which depends on size, but should not take longer than 4–5 minutes, they are ready. Take them out with a perforated spoon, put in a colander, drain, rinse with warm water, drain thoroughly again, add to the sauce, arrange chicken on top, heat through, and serve.

Coq au Vin

Cut the capon into portions. Reserve the liver. Brown the bird in hot butter. Gently fry the pork belly or bacon to make it yield its fat, but do not allow to dry out. Add onions and mushrooms. Cook for 5 minutes. Add chicken portions, pour 2 tablespoons brandy over them, and set alight. As soon as the flame subsides, add wine. Add stock to make enough liquid to cover, season well, add garlic and bouquet garni.

Bring to the boil, cover, and continue to cook in the oven pre-heated to 350 °F (180 °C) for 45 minutes or until tender. Remove from oven. Transfer chicken and garnish to a deep serving dish. Keep hot.

Strain the sauce, thicken with kneaded butter, blending it in small pieces.

Dice the liver, season with salt and pepper, and fry quickly in a teaspoon of butter. Drain and pound in a mortar, dilute with remaining brandy.

Bring the sauce to the boil, pour a thin trickle of the sauce into the liver, stirring constantly. Blend the liver mixture into the sauce, reheat but do not allow it to boil. Check seasoning, pour sauce over the chicken, garnish with croûtons, and serve.

To make croûtons, cut crustless slices of white bread into various shapes, triangles, hearts, half-moons, lozenges – or stamp them out with biscuit cutters – and fry in butter or oil until golden on both sides.

Chicken alla Cacciatora (Signora Dell'Omo's recipe)

4–6 Servings
1 frying chicken, jointed
salt and pepper
2 oz (50 g) flour
6 tablespoons alive oil
1 clove finely chopped garlic
1 medium-sized finely chopped onion
1–2 seeded and sliced green peppers
¼ tablespoon rosemary
4–6 finely chopped anchovy fillets
2 tablespoons wine vinegar
2 small bay leaves
½ pint (250 ml) red Chianti
3 tablespoons tomato paste
6 tablespoons chicken stock (or water)
4 oz (100 g) fresh sliced mushrooms
1 tablespoon chopped parsley

Trim the chicken portions. Season flour with salt and pepper and dip the chicken in it, lightly shaking off any surplus flour. Heat oil, add garlic and onion, fry together for a minute, add chicken. Brown over a high flame for 7–8 minutes. Add peppers, rosemary, and anchovy fillets. Cook over medium heat for a couple of minutes, stirring. Add vinegar, bay leaves, and wine.

Cook uncovered for 12–15 minutes to reduce the liquid by about a third.

Blend tomato paste with stock, pour over chicken, cover, reduce heat to low, cook for 15 minutes.

Add mushrooms, simmer for another 15 minutes sprinkle with parsley, and serve.

Boiled Chicken with Parsley Sauce, English Style

4–5 Servings
1 boiling fowl
1 quartered carrot
1 onion stuck with a clove
bouquet garni
12 oz (300 g) lean bacon in a piece
parsley sauce (p. 73)

Poach the chicken in enough water to cover, with carrot, onion, and bouquet garni. Bring the bacon to the boil in water, drain and cook with the chicken. When the chicken is done, remove and arrange on a heated serving dish. Garnish with boiled bacon cut in square pieces. Serve with parsley sauce.

Paella

6–8 Servings
3 tablespoons oil
1 jointed chicken
1 finely chopped onion
3 ripe tomatoes, peeled and chopped
1½ lb (750 g) rice
½ lb (200 g) runner beans
½ lb (200 g) peas
3 red peppers, seeded and sliced
1 small cooked or tinned crayfish,
cut in pieces
½ pint (250 g) peeled prawns
1 pint (½ litre) mussels
pinch saffron
2½ pints (1¼ litres) stock
1 teaspoon salt
½ teaspoon pepper

Heat the oil. Add chicken and brown lightly, add onion. When the onion is golden add tomatoes. Cook for a few minutes then put in the rice and simmer for 10 minutes. Add runner beans or peas, and cook for 5 minutes. Add peppers, crayfish, and any other seafood. Scrub mussels, rinse well, discard all open ones. Test carefully: they should shut tightly if given a sharp tap. Add to rice. Add the saffron to stock or water with a bouillon cube and pour into the pan. Season to taste and boil fast for 8 minutes. Reduce heat and simmer for 8 minutes. When the rice is cooked and all the water has been absorbed, put the paella in the oven for 5 minutes to give it a nice golden colour. Take it out of the oven and let it stand for a couple of minutes 'to settle' before serving.

Chicken Vindaloo

4 Servings
4 tablespoons butter
2–3 chopped cloves garlic
2 medium-sized chopped onions
2 tablespoons vindaloo paste (p. 180)
2 tablespoons lime (or lemon) juice
1 lb (¼ kg) chicken meat
water
salt

Heat the butter and fry the garlic and onions until soft. Add vindaloo paste and lime juice, stir and simmer very gently for 5 minutes, taking care not to burn the mixture. Cut the chicken into bite-size pieces, add to pan, mix well, moisten with ¼ pint (100 ml) water, cover, and simmer until tender. Do not allow the juices to dry out; add more liquid if necessary, though it should not be needed if the heat is kept really low. Taste for seasoning and serve.

Chicken and Rice Soufflé

4 Servings
8 oz (200 g) rice
2 pints (1 litre) chicken stock or
*   water with stock cube*
4 oz (100 g) butter
8 oz (200 g) diced chicken meat
2–3 tablespoons sherry
2 tablespoons Parmesan cheese
salt and pepper
4 egg yolks
4 stiffly beaten whites of egg

Cook the rice in chicken stock for 20 minutes.

Heat 1 oz (25 g) butter, lightly toss the chicken for half a minute, sprinkle with sherry and simmer for 3 minutes. Add chicken to rice, blend in cheese and remaining butter, adding and stirring it in small pieces. Allow to cool. Season to taste. Beat in the egg yolks, one by one. Mix well.

Fold in whites of egg, pour the mixture into a buttered soufflé mould and bake in a pre-heated moderate oven at 375 °F (190 °C) for 15 minutes. Serve at once.

Chicken Livers with Noodles

4 Servings
12 oz (300 g) chopped chicken livers
2 oz (50 g) olive oil
1–1½ chopped cloves garlic
½ lb (200 g) peeled, ripe tomatoes
4 oz (100 g) cooked green peas
salt and pepper
12 oz (300 g) noodles
grated cheese

Fry the livers in oil to brown on all sides. Add garlic and tomatoes. Cover and simmer on low heat for 20 minutes. Add peas, season to taste.

Cook the noodles, drain, put on a heated serving dish.

Pile the livers, peas, and the sauce on top and serve with grated cheese.

Chinese Chicken Livers with Prawns and Broccoli

4 Servings
1 lb (¼ kg) or one large packet
*   frozen broccoli*
salted water
8 oz (200 g) chicken livers, sliced
cornflour
2 tablespoons lard
salt
¼ oz (10 g) ginger, finely chopped
1 oz (25 g) spring onions, finely
*   chopped*

Boil the broccoli in a little salted water for 4 minutes and drain. Roll chicken livers in cornflour lightly and brown for 1 minute in 1 tablespoon lard. Remove from heat, season with salt, sprinkle with ginger, spring onions, and pepper.

Heat remaining tablespoon of lard, toss the mushrooms in it for 2 minutes. Add broccoli and cook together for 2 minutes.

Add liver with all its seasoning and prawns. Cook for 1 minute. Mix teaspoon of cornflour with soya sauce, dilute with 4 tablespoons water, blend into the pan. Cook for 1 minute and serve.

pepper
2 oz (50 g) fresh mushrooms, sliced
6 oz (150 g) peeled prawns
1 tablespoon soya sauce

Vegetable Dishes

Baby Onions in Sherry and Cream

Parboil the onions in a little salted water for 5 minutes, drain well, and put them in a shallow oven-proof dish.

Combine cream and cornflour, simmer gently stirring until the sauce thickens. Blend in half the butter adding and stirring it in small pieces. Check seasoning, add a grating of nutmeg and the sherry. Stir, pour the sauce over the onions.

Melt the remaining butter, mix with breadcrumbs, and sprinkle over the onions. Bake in a pre-heated oven at 350 °F (180 °C) for 18–20 minutes, to heat through and brown the top.

Serve with lamb or mutton.

4 Servings
1 lb (½ kg) peeled baby onions
salted water
4 oz (100 ml) single cream
2 teaspoons cornflour
2 tablespoons butter
pinch nutmeg
3–4 tablespoons sherry
3–4 tablespoons dry breadcrumbs

Ratatouille

In 2 tablespoons oil, lightly fry the onion and garlic. Fry the aubergine in a separate pan in 4 tablespoons oil until golden on all sides. Combine aubergine with onion and garlic, and add tomatoes, pimentos, zucchini, basil, lemon juice and salt, and freshly ground black pepper to taste. Simmer the ratatouille mixture for 25–30 minutes. Ratatouille can either be served at once, piping hot, or chilled.

4 Servings
olive oil
1 chopped onion
2 cloves minced garlic
1 peeled diced aubergine
5 oz (125 g) peeled, chopped tomatoes
2 pimentos seeded and cut in strips
3–4 small sliced zucchini (baby marrow)
1 teaspoon sweet basil
lemon juice
salt and freshly ground black pepper

Asparagus Quiche

Pastry

Heap the flour on a pastry board. Make a well in the centre, put in butter and salt, and work mixture with fingertips, adding a little cold water when necessary, until you have a smooth ball. If you are the lucky owner of a mixer, you will find this task much easier. Combine the pastry ingredients, without water, in a mixing bowl, having cut the fat into small pieces. (Avoid overfilling the bowl, to prevent flour spraying your kitchen.) Switch on the mixer to the lowest speed and let the blades mix the fat into the flour. Switch off and add cold water by hand.

6 Servings
10 oz (250 g) flour
3 oz (75 g) butter or other shortening
¼ teaspoon salt
cold water

Allow to rest several hours before rolling out. Meanwhile, prepare asparagus: snap off tough lower ends, scrape, wash in running water, tie in bundles, cook in salted water until just tender, and drain carefully.

Roll out the pastry and line a flan tin with it. Prick it with a fork on the bottom and sides. Bake in oven at 425 °F (220 °C) for 10 minutes.

Filling

Whisk the cream and eggs together until thoroughly blended. Season with salt and pepper. Pour the mixture into the partially cooked pastry shell. Bake 10 minutes longer.

Cut off the top 2 in. (5 cm) of the asparagus. Remove the quiche from the oven and stick the asparagus tips into the filling, tip sides up. Put back into the oven for 5 minutes or until the custard has set. Serve hot or cold. To freeze, cool, chill, unwrapped, then put in a suitable box and freeze. Avoid putting any heavy package on top of quiche.

To serve hot, put quiche in oven pre-heated to 350 °F (180 °C) and heat through.

To serve cold, thaw overnight in refrigerator.

2 lb (1 kg) asparagus
1 pint (½ litre) double cream
4 eggs
salt and pepper

3 Servings
1 lb (½ kg) cooked chopped spinach
3 tablespoons melted butter
4 oz (100 g) cooked rice
3 oz (75 g) grated cheese
salt and pepper
¼ teaspoon sugar
pinch grated nutmeg
1 teaspoon lemon juice

Rice and Spinach Timbale

Put the spinach in a mixing bowl.

Pour 2 tablespoons melted butter over rice and add to spinach. Add 2 oz (50 g) cheese, season with salt and pepper, sprinkle with sugar, nutmeg, and lemon juice and mix well.

Put the rice and spinach mixture into a well-buttered oven-proof dish and sprinkle the top with the remaining melted butter. Stand the dish in a bain-marie (pan of boiling water) and put in the oven pre-heated to 350 °F (180 °C). Bake for 30 minutes. Run a knife around the edge of the dish and turn the timbale out on to a heated serving dish.

Sprinkle with remaining grated cheese and serve.

6 Servings
6 red or green peppers
3 tablespoons rice
1 pint (½ litre) beef stock
10 oz (250 g) minced beef
1 oz (25 g) fresh breadcrumbs
1 onion
1 teaspoon paprika

Hungarian Stuffed Peppers

Wash the peppers and slice the stalk off them to obtain nice deep 'cups'. Scoop out seeds without damaging the shells. Cook rice for 5 minutes in stock and drain. Keep the stock. Add minced beef. Soak breadcrumbs in 1–2 tablespoons stock. Peel and finely chop onion. Add soaked breadcrumbs, onion, paprika, chopped parsley, salt and pepper to the rice and beef. Mix stuffing well and fill pepper shells.

Stand stuffed peppers upright in a buttered oven-proof dish. Blend tomato purée with the stock in which the rice was cooked and pour over the stuffed peppers.

Bake in a moderate oven at 375 °F (190 °C) for an hour, basting the peppers with the juices from time to time.

Serve hot or cold with sour cream.

2 tablespoons chopped parsley
salt, pepper
butter
1 tablespoon tomato purée
sour cream

Stuffed Mushrooms

Remove stalks from mushrooms and wash and carefully dry caps. Do not peel.

Blend chopped ham, crushed garlic and egg together. Dilute cornstarch in cognac and mix well into the ham mixture. Add salt and pepper to taste. Form into 24 little balls.

Place a ball of the ham mixture in each of the mushroom caps, pressing down slightly to give the final shape an even curve from edge to edge of the mushroom.

Place, ham side up, on a buttered baking tray and cook in a moderate oven at 375 °F (190 °C) for 30 minutes.

6 Servings
2 dozen medium-sized mushrooms
12 oz (300 g) chopped ham
1 clove garlic, crushed
1 egg
1 teaspoon cornstarch
1 teaspoon cognac
salt, pepper
butter

Stuffed Courgettes

Wash the courgettes, top and tail them, and cut them in half lengthwise. With a small spoon, scoop out the centre of the courgettes, so you are left with neat boat-shaped shells. Skin the onion and the clove of garlic and chop both up finely with the scooped-out courgette pulp. Add the minced beef, sweet basil, and salt and blend well with a wooden spoon. Fill the courgette shells with this mixture and place on an oiled baking tray. Cook in a moderately hot oven at 400 °F (200 °C) for 30 minutes.

Serve hot or cold.

The stuffing can also be made out of ham, or any left-over meat.

6 Servings
12 baby courgettes
1 small onion
1 clove garlic
4 oz (100 g) minced beef
1 teaspoon chopped sweet basil
1 teaspoon salt
oil for greasing baking tin

short pastry (p. 57)
1 lb (½ kg) leaf spinach
butter
4 oz (100 ml) cream
salt and pepper
pinch nutmeg

Spinach Tarts
Bake the tart cases.

Wash spinach, pick it over, discard tough stems, put in a pan with just the water left on the leaves after washing, cover and simmer for 3–4 minutes. Chop, rub through a sieve or pass through a blender. Mix with butter and cream, season with salt, pepper, and nutmeg. Blend well, fill the tart cases, put in the oven to heat through, and serve.

4–6 Servings
puff pastry
1 lb (½ kg) mushrooms, washed and
    sliced
2 tablespoons melted butter
1 tablespoon chopped parsley
pinch each of chopped chives and
    marjoram
4 oz (100 ml) chicken broth
4 tablespoons dry white wine
salt and pepper
1 egg yolk or 1 beaten egg

Swiss Mushroom Pie
Have the pastry ready for rolling out.

Grease a pie dish, put in mushrooms, and mix with the rest of the ingredients.

Roll out the pastry, cover the pie dish, make a hole in the centre to allow steam to escape during baking, brush with egg yolk or beaten egg seasoned with a pinch of salt, and bake in a hot oven pre-heated to 425 °F (220 °C) for 20 minutes.

Butters, Sauces, etc.

1 tablespoon finely chopped shallots
4 oz (100 ml) white wine
8 oz (200 g) bone marrow
4 oz (100 g) butter
1 tablespoon chopped parsley
salt and pepper
juice of ½ lemon

Bercy Butter
Cook the shallots in wine until the liquid is reduced by half and allow to cool. Dice the bone marrow, poach in salted water, and drain. Blend shallots with butter, parsley, seasoning, and lemon juice, add marrow, and serve on grilled steak or other meat.

6 oz (150 g) prawns
4 oz (100 g) butter

Prawn Butter
Cook the prawns in a court-bouillon (p. 180). Drain, pound in a mortar, shells and all. Put butter in a double saucepan, add prawns, and let the butter melt slowly. Stir to blend well, strain through a cloth, and store in a jar with a well-fitting lid. It will keep like ordinary butter.

2 oz (50 g) butter
2 oz (50 g) flour
1 pint (½ litre) milk or stock
salt and pepper

White Sauce
Melt the butter over low heat, stir in flour, and cook gently for 3 minutes, stirring all the time and without allowing to colour. Remove from heat, blend in half the liquid, return to heat, and cook, stirring vigorously. When the sauce thickens, add the rest of the liquid. Continue to simmer and beat the sauce until

the desired consistency is reached. Season, stir, and use at once.

Caper Sauce I

To white sauce add from 1 teaspoon to 1 tablespoon chopped capers, according to taste, and a few drops of vinegar from the capers.

½ pint (250 ml) white sauce
up to 1 tablespoon chopped capers

Caper Sauce II

Melt the butter over hot water. Chop the capers finely, add to butter, stir, and serve.

6 oz (150 g) butter
3 tablespoons capers

Horseradish Sauce

Grate horseradish finely, add sugar and vinegar, mix in cream – and the sauce is ready. It will be far superior in texture and flavour to any commercially manufactured article. Well worth the tears!

1 root horseradish
½ teaspoon sugar
1 teaspoon vinegar
4 oz (100 ml) cream

Mushroom Sauce

Toss the mushrooms in 1 tablespoon butter. Melt the rest of the butter, blend in flour, fry lightly, without allowing it to colour. Dilute gradually with stock, stirring constantly to ensure smoothness. Simmer for 7–8 minutes. Add mushrooms with their pan juices, stir, add cream, heat almost to boiling point, pour in Madeira, season to taste, sprinkle with dill, simmer without boiling for 2 minutes, and serve.

4 oz (100 g) sliced mushrooms
3 tablespoons butter
2 tablespoons flour
½ pint (250 ml) stock
4 oz (100 ml) cream
2 tablespoons Madeira (optional)
salt and pepper
1 teaspoon chopped dill (or parsley)

Tomato Sauce

Heat oil, fry onion until it becomes soft, add tomatoes, garlic, and basil, simmer slowly for half an hour, stirring from time to time. Add sugar, season with salt and pepper to taste, continue to simmer for 10 minutes.

4 tablespoons olive oil
1 finely chopped onion
1 lb (½ kg) peeled chopped tomatoes
pinch pounded garlic
1 teaspoon chopped basil
½ teaspoon sugar
pinch salt
freshly ground black pepper

Cream Gravy

Melt butter, stir in flour, cook together without allowing to brown. Gradually add cream, season, stir, simmer over hot water for 3–4 minutes until the sauce thickens, and serve at once.

2 tablespoons butter
4 tablespoons flour
½ pint (250 ml) single cream
salt and pepper

Court-Bouillon

Court-bouillon is an aromatized liquid for cooking fish and shellfish.

Salt-water court-bouillon: allow $1\frac{1}{2}$ teaspoons salt to a quart (1 litre) of water.

For poaching such fish as cod, perch, whitefish, haddock, salmon, etc. To preserve whiteness of fish, add 1 tablespoon vinegar (or lemon juice) per quart (1 litre) of water.

For lobster and other crustaceans court-bouillon is generally made of salt water, as above, flavoured with thyme and bay leaf, though sometimes thinly sliced onions, carrots, parsley, and peppercorns are added.

5–6 seeded fresh red chillis
$\frac{1}{2}$ in. (1 cm) slice of fresh green ginger
$1\frac{1}{2}$ teaspoons coriander
1 teaspoon cumin
1–2 cloves garlic
$\frac{1}{4}$ teaspoon powdered turmeric

Vindaloo Paste

Combine all ingredients and pound in a mortar or blend in a liquidizer to make a smooth paste. Use as directed. The amount is enough for one vindaloo dish for four persons. If desired, the amount of the ingredients can be multiplied and the paste kept in a jar with a tight-fitting lid.

2 lb (1 kg) redcurrants
$\frac{1}{2}$ pint (250 ml) water
sugar

Redcurrant Jelly

Simmer redcurrants with water until the skins break. Hang in thick muslin or a jelly bag over a bowl to catch the juice and leave to drip overnight.

Measure the juice and pour into preserving pan. For each pint ($\frac{1}{2}$ litre) of juice add 1 lb ($\frac{1}{2}$ kg) sugar. Stir it until dissolved completely. Boil until gelling point is reached. Start testing after 6–7 minutes.

Garnishes

Grilled Bacon Rolls

Use streaky bacon rashers. Remove rind and cut each rasher in half. Roll up firmly, skewer, and grill until crisp.

4 tablespoons self-raising flour
$\frac{1}{2}$ teaspoon salt
$\frac{1}{4}$ teaspoon cayenne pepper
1 egg
3 tablespoons milk
$\frac{1}{2}$ tablespoon melted fat
1 large tin whole kernel corn

Corn Fritters

Drain the corn.

Sift the flour with salt and pepper.

Beat the egg, add milk and melted fat, and stir the mixture into flour. Beat until the batter is smooth. Add corn, stir, and leave to stand for 10 minutes.

Heat fat, drop a tablespoon of the corn batter into hot fat, and fry gently, 2 minutes each side, turning once. Drain on absorbent paper and serve hot.

oil or fat for frying

Croûtons

To make croûtons, cut crustless slices of white bread into various shapes – triangles, hearts, half-moons, lozenges – or stamp them out with biscuit cutters – and fry in butter or oil until golden on both sides.

Fried Parsley

Wash parsley, dry, and divide into little sprigs. Put in a wire basket, plunge into sizzling fat for a few moments, drain, dry on a cloth, and serve as garnish.

Garlic Bread

Use French loaves. Score the bread, making deep incisions on a slant, but do not cut right through. Put generous helpings of garlic butter between each 'slice', reshape the loaf, put in the oven to heat and make crisp, and serve.

Desserts

Drambuie Moss

Dip the rim of 4 glasses first into egg white, then into granulated sugar to 'frost' them. Beat castor sugar and egg yolks until creamy, gradually whisk in fruit juices and Drambuie, and cook in a double boiler over hot water until frothy. Cool, pour into prepared glasses, chill. Before serving, pipe a border of cream on top.

4 Servings
a little egg white
granulated sugar
1 oz (25 g) castor sugar
3 egg yolks
3 teaspoons lemon juice
4 tablespoons orange juice
2 tablespoons Drambuie
4 oz (100 ml) whipped cream

Brandied Grapefruit

Slice grapefruits in half, cut to loosen segments, remove seeds and inner skins. Spread 2 tablespoons sugar over each grapefruit and sprinkle with brandy. Let stand for half an hour, then arrange on a baking tray and bake in the oven pre-heated to 350 °F (180 °C) until the top is bubbling. Serve very hot.

6 Servings
3 grapefruit
6 oz (150 g) demerara sugar
brandy

Caribbean Bananas

6 Servings
6 firm ripe bananas
butter
4 tablespoons sugar
a large glass of rum

Peel the bananas and place them in a buttered shallow oven dish. They should fit snugly. Dredge with sugar and sprinkle with rum. Bake in the oven at 375 °F (190 °C) until the bananas are tender.

Banana Cream

4 Servings
4 ripe bananas
3 oz (75 g) unsalted cream cheese
2 tablespoons cream
5 tablespoons sugar
5 tablespoons redcurrant jelly
chopped almonds

Crush ripe bananas with a fork until smooth. Add the cream cheese blended with the cream. Mix well and add the sugar. Mix again and spread on a small serving dish. Cover with the jelly and sprinkle with almonds. Serve very cold.

Egg-Nog Gâteau

10 Servings
1 tablespoon plain gelatine
4 tablespoons cold water
4 egg yolks
4 oz (100 ml) sherry
4 whites of egg
4 oz (100 g) sugar
1 pint (½ litre) cream
1 teaspoon vanilla essence
1 lb (½ kg or 1 packet) sponge
 fingers (p. 183)
12 almond macaroons, crumbled

Mix gelatine with cold water, dissolve over boiling water. Beat egg yolks and gradually add sherry, stirring constantly. Add gelatine, mix well. Beat egg whites until stiff, add sugar gradually, beating after each addition. Fold into yolk mixture, whip the cream, and blend in half of it together with vanilla. Line a mould with sponge fingers. Fill the mould with layers of egg-nog mixture, sprinkling each layer with macaroon crumbs. Chill overnight. Unmould and cover with the rest of the cream, whipped into a foam.

Tamara's Whisky Chocolate Pudding

6 Servings (or 4 for non-dieting
 gluttons)
12 sponge fingers (p. 183)
3 tablespoons cold strong black coffee
3 tablespoons whisky
8 oz (200 g) plain chocolate
5 eggs separated
2 oz (50 g) chopped roasted almonds

Arrange sponge fingers in a pretty glass serving dish. Sprinkle with mixed coffee and whisky so that the biscuits get pleasantly drunk without getting too sloppy.

Break up the chocolate into small pieces and melt very carefully in a basin over a pan of hot water (not boiling). When quite melted, take off the heat and beat in the egg yolks, one at a time. Whisk the egg whites to stiff peaks and gently fold into the chocolate mixture. Avoid beating. Pour mixture over sponge fingers and chill. Before serving, sprinkle top with chopped roasted almonds.

Tea Custard Cream

4 Servings
¾ pint (375 ml) double cream
¼ pint (125 ml) strong China tea
4 oz (100 g) sugar
3 egg yolks

Simmer the cream over low heat to reduce a little. Remove from the heat and stir in tea, sugar, and egg yolks, beating constantly. Strain through muslin into

four custard cups and put them in a pan of hot water.
Cook on top of the stove until the custard is set.

Coconut Pyramids

6 oz (150 g) desiccated coconut
4 oz (100 g) sugar
1 oz (25 g) potato flour
3 egg whites

Pre-heat oven to 350 °F (180 °C).

Combine coconut, sugar, and potato flour.

Whisk the egg whites until very stiff and fold into coconut mixture. Put mixture on a lightly greased baking sheet in spoonfuls, work into pyramid shapes, and bake for 35–40 minutes until crisp and lightly coloured.

Sponge Fingers

To make 2 dozen
3 eggs
4 oz (100 g) sugar
4 oz (100 g) plain flour
1 oz (25 g) butter
1 oz (25 g) castor sugar

Separate eggs and beat yolks with the sugar. Beat egg whites until stiff and fold into yolk and sugar mixture. Fold in flour. Fill a piping bag with this mixture and pipe 'fingers' on to a buttered floured baking tray. Leave for a few minutes, then sprinkle with castor sugar. Let sugar soak in for a few minutes then bake in a moderate oven pre-heated to 375 °F (190 °C) for 15 minutes.

Hazelnut Biscuits

12 oz (300 g) sugar
3 oz (75 g) ground hazelnuts
2 eggs
1½ tablespoons sherry
6 oz (150 g) pastry flour
2 oz (50 g) melted butter
3 oz (75 g) semi-sweet chocolate

Put sugar and hazelnuts into a bowl, add eggs and sherry, and mix well. Add flour, then stir in butter, which should be melted but not hot.

If you are going to serve the biscuits freshly made, skip the next paragraph and proceed to roll the dough into fingers.

To freeze, cool the mixture, shape into a roll, chill in refrigerator, then wrap closely in double foil and freeze. To use, thaw until you can handle the pastry.

Tear off small pieces of pastry, roll into little fingers. Pre-heat oven to 350 °F (180 °C).

Lightly grease a baking sheet, put hazelnut fingers on it, and bake for about 15 minutes. Remove and leave on a rack to cool. Melt chocolate in a bowl over hot water. Dip one end of each finger in it and stand upside-down to dry.

Lemon Meringue Pie

tart pastry
1 oz (25 g) cornflour
½ pint (250 ml) water
juice and grated rind of 2 lemons

Roll out tart pastry, line a flan tin, press down gently to make it fit and prevent formation of bubbles underneath, and crimp the edges. Prick the bottom of the

8 oz (200 g) sugar
¼ oz (15 g) butter
2 egg yolks
2 stiffly beaten egg whites
glacé cherries and angelica for
   decoration

2 lb (1 kg) pudding serves 10–12
10 oz (250 g) flour
5 oz (125 g) soft brown sugar
12 oz (300 g) shredded suet
1 teaspoon salt
8 oz (200 g) soft breadcrumbs
1 teaspoon mixed spice
pinch nutmeg
8 oz (200 g) sultanas
8 oz (200 g) seedless raisins
8 oz (200 g) currants
8 oz (200 g) chopped candied peel
8 oz (200 g) chopped blanched almonds
1 teaspoon grated lemon zest
5 eggs
¼ pint (250 ml) milk
3 tablespoons warmed brandy
1 teaspoon bicarbonate of soda

flan all over with a fork, cover with a circle of grease-proof paper, cut to fit the bottom, and fill with dried beans or rice. Bake in a hot oven at 400 °F (200 °C) for about 30 minutes or until the flan case becomes lightly browned. The beans can be stored and used again and again for the same purpose. Allow pastry case to cool. This part of the operation is known as baking a case 'blind'.

Mix cornflour with enough water to make a thin cream. Bring the rest of the water to the boil, pour on the cornflour and stir. Return mixture to saucepan, add lemon juice, and boil for 5 minutes, stirring constantly. Add half the sugar, butter, and grated lemon rind, cool slightly. Beat in the egg yolks one by one and pour the mixture into the flan case.

Gradually whisk sugar into the egg whites, pile on top of the lemon mixture, and bake in a slow oven at 300 °F (150 °C) for about 30 minutes, until the filling is set and the meringue crisp and a rich creamy colour. Decorate with cherries and angelica and serve cold.

Christmas Pudding

In a large mixing bowl, combine flour, sugar, suet, salt, breadcrumbs, spice, and nutmeg. Mix all the dried fruits, almonds, and lemon zest and add to the flour mixture. Beat the eggs, add all but 1 tablespoon of milk and stir well into the dry ingredients. Add brandy. Mix bicarbonate of soda with the remaining 1 tablespoon milk and stir well into the mixture. This amount of batter will make two 2 lb (1 kg) puddings or one 4 lb (2 kg) pudding.

For two puddings, butter two suitable pudding basins and divide the mixture equally. Cover with greaseproof paper and seal with aluminium foil or a well-tied cloth. Make sure no steam can escape from the puddings as they cook.

Fill two saucepans half full of water. When water boils, put in the puddings and cover. Boil for at least 8 hours. (For the larger pudding boil for at least 12 hours.)

To serve, unmould on to a serving dish, decorate with sprigs of holly, spoon brandy over the pudding, ignite, and carry, in blue flaming glory, into the darkened dining room. Serve with brandy butter, rum butter (p. 61), or cream.

Custard Pie

Roll out the pastry and line an 8 in. (20 cm) pie plate or tin with it. Take care not to stretch the pastry, to prevent shrinking. Press well down on to the plate or tin.

Beat eggs and sugar together. Pour in milk. Add vanilla and stir to dissolve sugar. Strain into prepared pastry. Sprinkle the top with a little grated nutmeg. Bake on the fifth shelf 'down' position for 15–20 minutes at 475 °F (240 °C) then for 15–20 minutes at 350 °F (180 °C).

6 oz (150 g) short-crust pastry (p. 57)
2 eggs
1 oz (25 g) sugar
½ pint (250 ml) milk
a few drops vanilla essence
grated nutmeg

Soufflé

Soufflés are very easy to prepare and make, especially if you have an electric mixer, which you will find makes light work of this.

Prepare the soufflé dish: oil the inside of the dish or grease it with clarified butter and pin or tie around it a collar of greased paper extending about 3 in. (8 cm) above the rim to support the soufflé as it rises.

Melt butter. Stir in flour and cook gently without colouring. Remove and gradually stir in milk. Return to heat and stir, until the mixture leaves the sides of the pan. Remove and cool a little. Beat in egg yolks, one at a time. Add sugar and essence. Fold in the egg whites, very stiffly beaten with the pinch of salt. Avoid overmixing.

Turn into prepared soufflé dish, half filling it, and run the tip of a knife round the inside of the dish.

Bake on second shelf 'down' position for 25 minutes at 400 °F (200 °C).

To remove the paper: unpin it or untie the string. Place a knife upright against the side of the dish, and pull the edge of the paper back over the blade to gently ease the collar off. Serve at once.

1 oz (25 g) butter
1 oz (25 g) plain flour
¼ pint (100 ml) milk
3 egg yolks
1 level tablespoon castor sugar
¼ teaspoon vanilla essence
4 egg whites
pinch of salt

Chocolate Soufflé

Add 2 oz (50 g) plain chocolate in small pieces to warm milk to dissolve.

Follow above recipe.

6 oz (150 g) short pastry (p. 57)
2 oz (50 g) glacé cherries
2 oz (50 g) butter or margarine
2 oz (50 g) castor sugar
1 large egg
2 drops almond essence
3 oz (75 g) sifted self-raising flour
pinch of salt
2 oz (50 g) blanched almonds
milk to mix

Cherry Almond Flan

Line a shallow 10 in. (25 cm) tin with the pastry. Place the cherries on it. Cream the butter and sugar and beat in the egg and almond essence. Fold in flour and salt. Spread the mixture evenly over cherries. Halve the almonds and arrange on top.

Bake on fourth shelf 'down' position for 35–40 minutes at 400 °F (200 °C).

Flaky Pastry

Using the same ingredients as for puff pastry, sift the flour and salt into a bowl. Divide the butter into four equal portions. Rub one of them into the flour to very fine crumbs.

Add the lemon juice and enough cold water to make a not-too-soft dough. Knead until very smooth.

Roll out to a long strip, keeping the edges as straight as possible. Mark the strip into thirds and flake the second portion of fat over two of these thirds. Fold the end uncovered piece over the centre third and bring the remaining third over on top of both. Press the sides and across the pastry with the rolling-pin to trap the air.

Put in the refrigerator for a few minutes to rest.

Roll out again, turning the dough half left or right and repeat the same process, using the third portion of fat. Put in the refrigerator again for a few minutes. Repeat the turning and rolling out and folding, using the remaining portion of fat. Wrap in greaseproof paper and leave in the refrigerator for at least an hour before using.

INDEX

Index to Recipes